Compendium of Over 2000 Jazz Pianists

ARNIE FOX

Trafford
PUBLISHING

Note for Librarians: a cataloguing record for this book that includes Dewey Decimal Classification
and US Library of Congress numbers is available from the Library and Archives of Canada. The
complete cataloguing record can be obtained from their online database at:
www.collectionscanada.ca/amicus/index-e.html
ISBN 1-4251-1848-8

Offices in Canada, USA, Ireland and UK
This book was published *on-demand* in cooperation with Trafford Publishing. On-demand
publishing is a unique process and service of making a book available for retail sale to the public
taking advantage of on-demand manufacturing and Internet marketing. On-demand publishing
includes promotions, retail sales, manufacturing, order fulfilment, accounting and collecting
royalties on behalf of the author.

Book sales for North America and international:
Trafford Publishing, 6E–2333 Government St.,
Victoria, BC v8t 4p4 CANADA
phone 250 383 6864 (toll-free 1 888 232 4444)
fax 250 383 6804; email to orders@trafford.com
Book sales in Europe:
Trafford Publishing (uk) Limited, 9 Park End Street, 2nd Floor
Oxford, UK OX1 1HH UNITED KINGDOM
phone 44 (0)1865 722 113 (local rate 0845 230 9601)
facsimile 44 (0)1865 722 868; info.uk@trafford.com
Order online at:
trafford.com/06-3328

10 9 8 7 6 5 4 3

Dedicated to
Stephan Peiffer

and the memory Of
Bernard Peiffer

Foreword
Don Glanden

Jazz pianists everywhere pursue their art in small clubs and bars, where they are often free to develop improvisational skill but seldom in the presence of an attentive audience. The opportunities to perform in concert halls, or in clubs dedicated solely to jazz, are coveted but are much too rare for the majority of jazz musicians. Much of the development in the playing of individual musicians occurs with few listeners sharing in the creative experience. Of course, a musician doesn't require the presence of an attentive audience to enter into a deep musical experience. However, when there are people present who listen intently, are moved by the music, and respond, another dimension of involvement is added- a rewarding one that enriches the player and listener alike.

Whenever Arnie Fox goes to listen in a club, he raises the level of communication between performer and audience. His extraordinary focus on the content of the music encourages musicians to experience a high level of engagement, regardless of the setting. He often takes notes, asks questions about repertoire, and makes many observations about style, technique, rhythmic approach, and historical perspective. I'm sure that countless jazz pianists (including myself) have been encouraged to look up from the instrument and see Arnie with his wife, Diana, listening to every note. One such pianist, the great Bernard Peiffer, inspired *Compendium of Over 2000 Jazz Pianists*. Peiffer's remarkable playing at the Woodland Inn near Philadelphia in 1961 stunned Arnie, and motivated him to produce a work that would bring much deserved attention to many extraordinary but lesser know pianists.

With the explosion of information on the Internet, easy access to an extensive amount of musical documentation has become a reality. Discographies, biographies, career itineraries, and critical documentation through archived reviews are available to serious researchers, jazz aficionados, and casual fans. What makes *Compendium of Over 2000 Jazz Pianists* special is its personal approach and the underlying motivation of the author. The book provides an extensive list of jazz pianists, each of whom has been researched personally by Arnie Fox, who invested hundreds of hours of critical listening to this project. Also included is the recommendation of a single representative recording for each pianist. The book fulfills the author's objective, to provide readers with an introduction to the work of many creative musicians that may have been overlooked in the reader's own listening experience.

Compendium of Over 2000 Jazz Pianists will be a welcome addition to the libraries of jazz piano aficionados. It is a wonderful source for motivated listeners looking to expand their knowledge of the many musicians who have contributed to the art of jazz piano. Thank you, Arnie Fox, for your commitment to this project, and for your desire to share your enthusiasm and dedication to jazz with others.

Don Glanden
Division Head, Graduate Jazz Studies
Coordinator, Piano Studies
The University of the Arts
Philadelphia, PA
January 28, 2007

To create a database for jazz pianists is an ongoing process since there are more and more jazz pianists coming onto the scene every day. This makes the task an impossible project, but one that I will attempt to tackle with further compendiums. I want to make everyone aware of the great talent that is out there and has not been exposed due to the lack of marketing and or financial resources to have their works known.

By listing the various jazz pianists and their albums and CD's, I hope that every musician will seek out their work to learn from their unusual and individualistic styles so that they can experience their unique talent as I have done. Most musicians are unable to concentrate on their profession exclusively due to the lack of "gigs" available and the low pay. Therefore, they must have another source of income in order to sustain themselves in this creative art form.

When I first started this project, I never realized how much talent there was out there. My main purpose is to make you aware of the various artists and you can determine which ones suit your fancy. I personally relate to those artists who keep the melody line in tact, but I can appreciate all forms of jazz when I listen to the album more than once and therefore acquire a taste for other forms of piano playing other than the "Tatum" style.

The database is merely a guide to the many artists out there. It is in no way a list of their best albums. It is merely a reference point to look up a particular artist. Most of these records can be purchased at a record store, but many must be found at out-of-print record shops.

Some that are listed can be ordered at www.cdbaby.com. You may also find out that many artists are selling their CD's through their own website. The artist makes more money this way and usually discounts the CD's purchased depending upon the quantity sold.

The following pianists have great technique and style and are among my many favorites (in alphabetical order): Toshiko Akiyoshi, Joe Albany, Monty Alexander, Kenny Barron, Gordon Beck, Richie Beirach, Armand Boatman, Claude Bolling, Joanne Brackeen, Evans Bradshaw, Dave Brubeck, Ray Bryant, John Bunch, Joe Bushkin, Eddie Cano, Barbara Carroll, Bill Charlap, Herman Chittison, Nat "King" Cole, Cy Coleman, Chick Corea, Johnny Costa, Stanley Cowell, Blossom Dearie, Lorraine Desmarais, Dorothy Donegan, Kenny Drew, Duke Ellington, Bobby Enriquez, Bill Evans, Don Ewell, Irving Fields, Tommy Flanagan, Russ Freeman, Don Friedman, Dave Frishberg, Red Garland, Erroll Garner, Don Glanden, Conley Graves, Johnny Guarnieri, Herbie Hancock, Sir Roland Hanna, Barry Harris, Gene Harris, Hampton Hawes, Earl "Fatha" Hines, Dick Hyman, Calvin

Jackson, Hank Jones, Oliver Jones, Dick Katz, Diana Krall, Donald Lambert, Michel Legrand, Keith MacDonald, Adam Makowicz, Tania Maria, Dave McKenna, John Mehegan, Thelonius Monk, Tete Montoliu, Dudley Moore, Dick Morgan, Morris Nanton, Peter Nero, Phineas Newborn, Jr., Walter Norris, Bernard Peiffer, Oscar Peterson, Bud Powell, Andre Previn, Mark Randall, George Shearing, Johnny "Hammond" Smith(organist), Derek Smith, Paul Smith, Martial Solal, Art Tatum, Billy Taylor, Fats Waller, Dick Wellstood, Jesssica Williams, John Williams, Mary Lou Williams, Jack Wilson, Teddy Wilson, Denny Zeitlin and Pablo Ziegler. These are the artists I listen to the most.

One evening as I was having dinner at a local restaurant, there was a pianist next to me playing an upright piano. I could not believe what I heard nor could I follow his hands across the keyboard. They were a complete blur! His technique was astounding and I said to my wife, "Diana," Do you see what he's doing?" She said, "Arnie please eat your dinner before it gets cold". I can't remember if I ever finished the meal. The pianist was Bernard Peiffer! After hearing him, I searched out the few albums that he made. I tried to find out where he was performing next. He appeared at the Painted Bride on South Street in Philadelphia. There was a small crowd there and everyone was in awe of him. He appeared in other locations in the Philadelphia, PA area such as Cheltenham High School, where many of his students were there to cheer him on. I also saw him at the University of the Arts and a little night spot called The Borgia Café along with his bass player, Al Stauffer. I became obsessed with him and everyone that I spoke to never even heard of him! Most jazz books don't even mention his name! He was a cross between Art Tatum, Garner and Oscar Peterson all rolled into one.

When I asked my piano teacher who his favorite jazz pianist was, he replied "there is only one and that one is Tatum!" I then mentioned Bernard Peiffer and he said he never heard of him! I loaned him a Peiffer album and he became an immediate convert. He also, could not believe what he heard. After Peiffer died, I decided to write a compendium of jazz pianists and then I discovered Jessica Williams!! What a beautiful and talented pianist. You can purchase her CD's through her own website, jessicawilliams. com and learn much about the music business plus.

I then heard from my daughter Pamela that there is an independent website, www.cdbaby.com, that promotes many unknown artists. Much to my surprise, I found out that a new CD titled "Formidable" just came out produced by Stephan Peiffer, (Bernard Peiffer's son) and Don Glanden (another fabulous pianist once a student of Bernard) on Bernard Peiffer! I immediately ordered the CD and got in touch with Stephan and Don Glanden. I was so happy to talk to both of them about my experiences with Bernard Peiffer and the ten hours of live tape that I had of him.

I then went to see Don Glanden perform at Sullivan's Steakhouse in Delaware and loaned him all the information and tapes on Bernard. Don typed up the interview my wife and I had copied from the Philadelphia Public Library that was translated by Marc Kniebihler, a friend of my wife. Enclosed is a copy of that translation.

This database will cover the obscure and rarely publicized players. This book is a labor of love since I have always wanted to write a book on piano players but I felt that I didn't have the training. I now realize that even though I am self taught, I have been exposed to so many different types of players that I feel that I am just as qualified as any other jazz or pop critic. Whether I have enough information, that will always be a problem since there will always be a new "Tatum" or and old "Tatum" still to be discovered. So that rather than wait, I feel the time is right for me to let all music lovers know all the jazz piano players of whom I am aware.

Questions that I would like answered:

Why doesn't most of the public listen to the piano player at a club or restaurant?

Don't the patrons of the club or restaurant realize that the pianist would like to be acknowledged by applause?

Do they take him for granted?

Why doesn't the club owner tune the piano regularly or why doesn't he tune it at all?

Why doesn't the hostess ask the customer if they want to

sit near the piano player? If they want to talk only and not listen, sit them as far away from the piano player as possible!

Why don't they play the "good jazz" on the radio stations other than jazz such as easy listening?

Why aren't there awards on TV for best jazz players like they do for rock, soul and pop?

Can't we have general music courses in high school to educate the students as to what "good jazz" players there are?

When are people going to wake up and listen to real musicians?

How many of you have ever purchased a jazz CD or album(not downloaded)?

Why can't newspapers review jazz CD's?

Why are so many columnists who are music critics completely uninformed about jazz?

Why can't the TV talk shows have guests that are jazz musicians?

It would be my fantasy if the above questions were answered the way that I want them to be!

Let's have an "American Idol" for jazz musicians. The public must be made aware of real talent! There really is other music besides rock and rap.

The bands on TV talk shows are hardly ever featured and play for three minutes if they're lucky and that's only to introduce the host!

How to use the database:

1 Try one of the pianists listed. If you like the artist, see if there are reviews in the Penguin Guide, Downbeat or any other jazz magazine.

2 Go to cdbaby.com to order any on the list. Review any numbers. Try out any other artists to see if their style appeals to you.

3 If you really get hooked on jazz pianists, go to tomlord. com and order his complete discography which covers every musician not just pianists. The artist that you seek will probably be listed unless he or she is very new on the scene. I found his discography to be most useful in order to get the full picture of what the artist has recorded.

4 Try out any artists that have their own website.

5 Finally, support the musicians by attending any of their concerts. Let your friends know there is a lot of talent out there yet to be discovered.

Enjoy the database because I only have scratched the surface of the number of jazz pianists that made a record or CD. What about all those great musicians that have never recorded?

My Favorite Albums and CD's—
Alphabetical Order

1 Alexander, Monty-Threesome, SN 1152, SoulNote LP-1985

2 Basie, Count-Kansas City-Count Basie 5, 2312-126, Pablo LP-1984

3 Boatman, Armand-Live at Gregory's, PR 7166, PAUSA LP-1984

4 Bolling, Claude-Suite for Flute and Jazz Piano-M33233, CBS LP-1975

5 Brackeen, Joanne-Invitation-J.B.Trio-FLP.41044-Freedom LP-1976

6 Bradshaw, Evans-Look Out For Evans Bradshaw!, 12-263, Riverside LP

7 Busch, Lou-Lazy Rhapsody, L.B. his piano & orch., T-1072, Capitol LP

---

8 Bushkin, Joe-I Get A Kick Out of Porter, T-1030, Capitol LP

9 Cano, Eddie-Here Is The Fabulous E.C., R-6055, Reprise LP

10 Caroll, Barbara- At the Piano, DS-847, Discovery LP-1980

11 Castro, The Brothers- Recorded Live at Harrah's Tahoe, T2015, Capitol LP

12 Cole, Nat "King"-The Complete Early Transcriptions-Vol.1-4, Vintage Jazz Classics- 4 CD's

13 Costa, Johnny-Flying Fingers, Chiaroscuro CD-1990-1991

14 Cowell, Stanley-Live at Maybeck Recital Hall, Vol.5, Concord CD-1990

15 Davis, Sammy Jr.- S.D. Jr. at Town Hall, DL-78841,Decca LP-1958

16 Dearie, Blossom-Chez Wahlberg, Part One-Vol.IX, BMD109, Daffodil-1985

17 Desmarais, Lorraine-The L.D.Trio, JZ100 Jazzimage LP -1985

18 Donegan, Dorothy-D.D. Live! T-1155-Capitol LP

19 Ellington, Duke-D.E- Capitol Small Groups, Mosaic 5CD's

20 Enriquez, Bobby-Live! In Tokyo, GNPS2161, GNP Crescendo LP-1982

21 Evans, Bill-Affinity, BSK-3293, Warner Bros.LP-1978

22 Feinstein, Michael-Live At The Algonquin, PRO-101, Parnassas LP-1986

23 Fitzgerald, Ella-Sings The George & Ira Gershwin Songbook, 2615-063, Verve 5LP's

24 Freshmen, Four-Voices in Latin, T-922, Capitol LP

25 Friedman, Don-Invitation- D.F.Trio, Progressive CD-1978

26 Frishberg, Dave-Live at Vine Street F-9638, Fantasy LP-1984

27 Garner, Erroll-Concert By The Sea, CL-883, Columbia LP-1956

28 Gershwin, George-Gershwin Plays Gershwin-The Piano Rolls, Elektra Nonesuch CD

29 Goodman, Benny-The Complete Capitol Small Group Recordings of B.G., Mosaic 4CD's

30 Gorme, Eydie- Eydie Swings The Blues, ABC-192, ABC LP

31 Grappelli, Stephane- S.G.Plays Jerome Kern, GR-1032,GRP LP-1987

32 Graves, Conley-Piano Dynamics-The C.G.Trio, DL-8412, Decca LP

33 Hancock, Herbie-Gershwin's World, Verve CD-1998

34 Hanna, Roland-Perugia-Live At Montreux '74, AL-1010, Arista LP-1984

35 Harris, Barry-Live at Maybeck Recital Hall-Vol.12,

Concord CD

36 Harris, Gene-Live at Otter Crest, Concord CD-1981

37 Hines, Earl- E.H. Plays George Gershwin, CJ-31, Classic Jazz 2LP's-1973

38 Holiday, Billy-The Complete B.H. on Verve 1945-1959

39 Hyman, Dick- Genius at Play-Improvised Jazz Piano

40 Jackson, Calvin-Jazz Variations on Movie Themes, R-2007, Reprise LP

41 Jamal, Ahmad-Chicago Revisited/Live at Joe Segal's Show, Telarc CD-1992

42 Jones, Hank-Solo Piano, SJL-1124, Savoy LP-1956

43 Jones, Oliver-The Many Moods of O.J., Just 3, Justin Time LP-1984

44 Kral, Roy-Jackie & Roy-We've Got It: The Music of Cy Coleman, DS-907, Discovery LP-1984

45 Lambert, Donald-Giant Stride-D.L. & His Harlem Piano, BJ18001, Solo Art LP

46 Lawton, Tom-Al Stauffer Trio-Things Ain't What They Used To Be, Plattonic CD-1993

47 Makowicz, Adam-From My Window, CRS-1028, Choice LP-1980

48 Maria, Tania-T.M.et Niels-Henning Orsted Pedersen, ACV-130, Accord LP-1979

49 McKenna, Dave-Live at Maybeck Recital Hall, Vol.2, Concord CD-1989

50 McPartland, Marian-M.P. at The Hickory House, Savoy Jazz CD-1953

51 Mehegan, John-How I Play Jazz Piano, MG-12076, Savoy LP-1957

52 Moore, Dudley-The D.M.Trio, PS-558, London LP-1969

53 Nanton, Morris-Preface: The M.N.Trio, PR-7345, Prestige LP

54 Nero, Peter-Piano Forte-The Magnificent Piano of P.N., LPM-2334, RCA LP-1961

55 Newborn, Phineas Jr.-While My Lady Sleeps, LPM-1474, RCA LP-1957

56 Norris, Walter-Live at Maybeck Recital Hall, Vol.4, Concord CD-1990

57 O'Neal, Johnny-Soulful Swinging, Just A Memory CD-1985

58 Peiffer, Bernard-Modern Jazz For People Who Like Original Music, LLP-1006, Laurie LP

59 Peterson, Oscar-O.P. In Russia, 2625-711, Pablo 2LP's

60 Peterson, Oscar-Motions & Emotions – three originals-Vol.1 & 2, MPS 2CD's

61 Piazzolla, Astor-Gary Burton-A.P. Reunion, Concord CD-1996

62 Piazzolla, Astor-Pablo Ziegler Quintet for New Tango, RCA CD-1999

63 Powell, Bud- B.P. Jazz Giant, MGV-8153, Verve Cleff LP

64 Previn, Andre-Shelly Manne & His Friends: "My Fair Lady", M-3527, Contemporary LP-1956

65 Randall, Mark- M.R. At The Café Royal, MR001, Mirth LP-1984

66 Raney, Sue- S.R. Sings The Music of Johnny Mandel with the Bob Florence Trio, DS-875, Discovery LP-1982

67 Richards, Ann-Two Much! A.R. & Stan Kenton, T-1495, Capitol LP

68 Shearing, George- Shearing on Stage!, T-1187,Capitol LP

69 Shearing, George-Top Drawer-G.S.-Mel Torme, CJ-219, Concord LP-1983

70 Solal, Martial-Nothing But Piano, 5D-064D, MPS LP-1975

71 Tatum, Art-The Tatum Solo Masterpieces, 2625-703, Pablo 13LP's

72 Tronsco, David-Meant To Be- featuring Eddie Cano, D2-001, Dii LP

73 Vaughan, Sarah-How Long Has This Been Going On? 2310-821, Pablo LP-1978

74 Waller, Fats-Fats Waller Memorial, 730570/74, RCA 5LP's

75 Walton, Cedar -Maybeck Recital Hall Series Vol. 25, Concord CD-1992

76 Wellstood, Dick- D.W.Live at Café des Copains, DDA 1003, Unisson LP-1985

77 Werner, Kenny-Form and Fantasy, Double-Time Records CD-2000

78 Williams, Jessica-Maybeck Recital Hall Series, Vol.21, Concord CD-1992

79 Wilson, Jack-Innovations, DS-777, Discovery LP-1977

80 Wilson, Teddy- Mr.Wilson -The Fabulous T.W. At The Piano, CL-748, Columbia LP

81 Wonder, Stevie- Stevie Wonder's Journey Through The Secret Life of Plants, T13-371C2, Tamla 2LP's-1979

82 Young, John-J.Y.Trio-Themes and Things, LP-692, Argo LP-1961

83 Zeitlin, Denny-Maybeck Recital Hall Series, Vol.27, Concord CD-1992

Compilations

The Greatest Jazz Recordings of All Time-Vol.9-12-Jazz Masters of the Keyboard-Vol.1-Franklin Mint 4LP's

The Greatest Jazz Recordings of All Time-Vol.49-52-Jazz Masters of the Keyboard-Vol.2-Franklin Mint 4LP's

The Greatest Jazz Recordings of All Time-Vol.77-80-Piano Stylists 1927-1980-Franklin Mint 4LP's

MPS Piano Highlights, MPS 2CD's

The Complete Master Jazz Piano Series, Mosaic 4CD's

The Complete Jazz at The Philharmonic, Verve 10CD's

Commodore Piano Anthology, GRP CD

About CD Baby

Who/What are we?

CD Baby is a little online record store that sells CDs by independent musicians.

[In-de-pen-dent]: (adj.) Not having sold one's life, career, and creative works over to a corporation.]

We're just a few people in a cool Portland, Oregon, CD warehouse that looks like a playground. We listen to every CD we sell before we sell it, so we can help you find other albums you'll like.

We only sell CDs that come directly from the musicians. No distributors. Musicians send us CDs. We warehouse them, sell them to you, and pay the musicians directly.

Cool thing: in a regular record deal or distribution deal, musicians only make $1-$2 per CD, if they ever get paid by their label. When selling through CD Baby, musicians make $6-$12 per CD, and get paid weekly.

In business, and thriving, since March 1998. We're the largest seller of independent CDs on the web.

History

I was just selling my own CD in 1997, making my living by touring and doing sessions, and asked some fellow musicians if they'd like me to sell their CD, too. It was supposed to be a hobby. (Making music was my real career!)

For the first year, CD Baby was just me. I'd put the day's orders in my backpack and ride my bike down to the post office...

But then friends told friends, and now my little hobby has sold over $25 MILLION in independent CDs to people around the world.

Current Numbers

153,386 artists sell their CD at CD Baby.

2,739,196 CDs sold online to customers.

$34,257,817.28 paid to artists.

CD Baby Privacy Policy

We NEVER give or sell your personal info to any other company –EVER! (No not even your email address!)

Only the musician whose CD you buy will know who you are.

If you don't even want the musician to know about you, just say so at the bottom of your order form.

Your credit card info is never stored, and never seen by anyone. We don't store it in your permanent customer info. The card number is erased immediately after the sale, for extra protection. There is nothing of yours to steal.

Yes this means you'll have to type your card number again when you return, but we hope you appreciate the extra safety and privacy it gives you.

Tech Things

Our servers are running FreeBSD, Apache, PHP, and MySQL.

No Microsoft products were used in the creation of this website.

Full 128-bit secure SSL connection protects all of your private information from snooping eyes. Our secure certificate issued by Thawte-a division of Verisign.

We try to stay HTML4.0 compliant. No special web browsers needed. (I recommend the FireFox and Opera web browsers for their speed and standards.)

CD Baby website (front end and back end) made by me-Derek Sivers. It's my favorite hobby.

Most important of all...

You can reach us during Pacific west-coast business hours at (503) 595-3000 or email @cdbaby.com anytime.

Bibliography

The All Music Guide to Jazz 4th Edition, edited by Vladimir Bogdanov, Chris Woodstra, and Stephen Thomas Erlewine.

American Musicians: 56 Portraits in Jazz, by Whitney Balliett.

American Musicians II: Seventy-Two Portraits in Jazz, by Whitney Balliett.

The Biographical Encyclopedia of Jazz by Leonard Feather & Ira Gitler.

Encyclopedia of Jazz, by Leonard Feather (and co-authors).

Jazz Portraits, by Len Lyons and Don Perlo.

CD Baby Website-permission from Derek Sivers to reproduce "About CD Baby"

The New Grove Dictionary of Jazz, edited by Barry Kernfeld.

Jazz for Dummies by Dirk Sutro.

The Penguin Guide to Jazz on CD Fifth Edition by Richard Cook & Brian Morton.

The Jazz Discography by Tom Lord- Version 6.0(order thru www.tomlord.com)

The Fifty Greatest Jazz Piano Players of All Time by Gene Rizzo.

88 The Giants of Jazz Piano by Robert L. Doerschuk.

The Virgin Encyclopedia of Jazz Revised and Updated compiled and edited by Colin Larkin.

Jessica Williams website used, with permission from Jessica Williams, to reproduce her discography

Wikipedia, the free encyclopedia, used for the biography of Jessica Williams.

Discography of Bernard Peiffer

1 Bernard Peiffer Plays Cole Porters Can-Can, LLP-1108, Laurie LP-1960

2 Bernard Peiffer- "Piano A La Mood", DL-9203, Decca LP-1958

3 Bernard Peiffer- Modern Jazz for People Who Like Original Music, LLP-1006, Laurie LP-1959

4 Bernie's Tunes Featuring Bernard Peiffer, MG-36080, Emarcy LP

5 The Astounding Bernard Peiffer/Presenting The Bernard Peiffer Trio, DL-8626, Decca LP-1957

6 Le Most featuring Bernard Peiffer, MG-26036, Emarcy 10"LP

7 New Sound at the "Boeuf Sur Le Toit-Henri Renaud et son Orchestre, BS-6831, Blue Star LP-1952

8 Don Byas in Paris, PR-7598, Prestige LP-1946 & 1949

9 The Pied Peiffer of the Piano-Bernard Peiffer, DL-9218, Decca LP-1959

10 Bernard Peiffer & His Jazz Piano Plays Prelude, Fugue & Trio on Lullaby of Birdland, 623210, International Polydor LP-1965

11 Jazz at Saint-Germain Des Pres (Don Byas et ses rythmes & B.Peiffer et son trio), MGV-8119, Verve Cleff LP(one side, Don Byas, other side Bernard Peiffer)

12 Jazz in Paris-Bernard Peiffer-La vie en rose, Gitanes-65-1952 & 1953, CD

13 Jazz in Paris-Modern Jazz at St.Germain, Gitanes-48-1954(CD re-issue of MGV-8119, Verve Cleff LP)

14 Don Byas 1947-1951 (3 numbers by Peiffer), Classics 1239, CD

15 Rex Stewart-1948-1949, Classics, CD (4 numbers)

16 James Moody-1949-CD

17 Sidney Bechet-Concert "Victoria Hall", Geneve, Photastic(Swd) NOST7602 entitled "The Paris Jazz Festival" LP-1949

18 The Edward's Jazz Band/The Saratoga Jazz Hounds: Bill Coleman and Don Byas, Clifford CRJCD1002 (CD)-1949

19 Bernard Peiffer Plays Standards, Jazz in Paris (re-issue of Piano et Rhythmes, 84008, Barclay Disques-1954 with additional numbers not on LP)

20 The New Glenn Miller Orchestra in Hi Fi directed by Ray

McKinley, LSP-1522, RCA LP-1957

21 Bernard Peiffer-Formidable...!-2005 Manege Music Productions LLC-CD

Bernard Peiffer

Interview with French Jazz Magazine (Jazz Mag)

(Given on Bernard's return to France for Antibes festival, probably 1966)

JAZZMAG   **Bernard Peiffer, why did you leave France in 1954?**

BERNARD PEIFFER   **At the time, I thought not much was going on there about jazz. I thought jazz was under rated there. Also, I was interested about America. I wanted to see the country of jazz. Not about jazz business because it's not the point of view of the artists. I wanted to see the life of people who created jazz. Just like good wine, you have to drink it where it's made.**

JM **Why did you come back?**

BP **I wanted to come back for quite some time, but I didn't have the opportunity because of engagements in some jazz clubs. Then I got the opportunity so here I am.**

JM **When you got to the U.S., the critics were good to you!**

BP **They were not indifferent. Some said I was using my technique to express my ideas, others said that my ideas, were backed by my technique. But they all made the fundamental mistake of comparing me with other artists. If an artist has something to say, you should criticize what he is saying and not try to look where it's coming from. Music is a big ladder and each musician is one of its steps. If Bach didn't exist, maybe we wouldn't play what we're playing now, each artist is influenced by _his_ predecessor.**

JM **About yourself, people wrote in the U.S. "This is the successor of Tatum..."**

BP **It's a great honor for me but I said "Leave Art Tatum alone because for me he is my daddy." And who were Tatum's predecessors? Fats Waller? James P. Johnson? What you have to do is underline what the artist is creating , what new things he is bringing. I heard someone say _that_ Charles Lloyd takes after Coltrane. It's ridiculous.**

JM **he came after him...**

BP **No, there's no relation.**

JM **When you came to the U.S., did you work right away?**

BP Two months *later*, at "L'Embers" it was the most famous jazz restaurant, I started with George Shearing, he helped me a lot.

JM What was the most surprising thing for you the first night at "L' Embers"?

BP The noise, I was *beginning* to see how impolite people were toward the artist, that's why I got into concerts.

JM Did you get offers to be a sideman?

BP Yes, when my *agent* was the "Willard Alexander Office." One time they called to ask me if I wanted to play with the Glenn Miller Band at the Pennsylvania state jail. I was worried but I accepted. I played with them for two weeks. They wanted to keep me but I got tired of it, the music arrangements were too old *fashioned*. It was the opposite of what I wanted to do.

JM Was that your only experience as a sideman?

BP No, I replaced Eddie Costa in the Woody Herman Quintet. It was good because there were Nat Adderly, Chubby Jackson, and my ex-drummer Jimmy Campbell. I didn't stay very long because I was signed up for some concerts. I also played shortly in Philadelphia. These were concerts of an hour or two, sometimes in the morning.

JM Were you always well received?

BP Oh yes, the kids liked it. I was explaining to them how I was playing.

JM In the American jazz circle you were well accepted, you, a Frenchman?

BP The roots of jazz are American but most people agree with its universal form. What else could you do? If you do a blindfold test, an American musician could not tell you who is playing: a white, a black, an American or a French.

JM Did you have problems finding good rhythm musicians for your style of music?

BP A band works well when everybody gets along with one another. It doesn't mean that two great talents can always play together. Sometimes they can destroy each other. Personally, I didn't *have* much trouble. I try to be comfortable by making other musicians feel comfortable. I respect my ideas and the *ones* of others. If it doesn't work we split.

JM The two bass players who played the most with you are Chuck Andrus and Gus Nemeth...

BP Yes, I discovered Gus Nemeth in 1958. Blossom Dearie presented him to me. I hired him, in the beginning he was a little young, so I *shaped* him to my ideas and we worked good things together.

JM And Chuck Andrus?

BP *That* was before. He is good for Woody Herman style but not so much for mine.

JM **Why?**

BP **It's not a matter of quality. We have different musical *points* of view. For me a bass player shouldn't just give the tempo, he should do things like Scott La Faro. I want to get inspired by the bass player, that's the time *when* there's a good exchange. I never considered my musicians as followers but as partners.**

JM **You like good music. What is for you bad music?**

BP **I think rock'n'roll is the disgrace(shame)of music. I don't understand *its existence*. It's like kid stuff. It's like a disease.**

JM **What's striking with Martial Solal is his desire to construct a coherent work where each piece *fits* into an ensemble. Do you feel the same?**

BP **No, I cannot strip my work to give *it* a pure *central point*. If one day I want to write a piece, I will take my time. I will retouch it, and I wouldn't be the only one, Bach did it and Beethoven and Chopin.**

JM **Maybe you prefer "*generasite*" over style. You'd rather give yourself totally, with your weak points even if it's not the purest of style.**

BP **Music is big. It's been there for *thousands* of years. And it will continue. Music is space and we live in space. It moves, it flies, it's good, it's bad, it's violent, it's sad. For me it's like theatre, a reflection of life.**

JM **Did you like the welcome you got from the public in Antibes?**

BP **I don't know because I don't pay attention to what goes on in the crowd. Sometimes my musicians *say* "We have to go back, the crowd is asking for you." I don't even listen if people are clapping or not.**

JM **In any case, at Antibes your time was short.**

BP **Yes, it was not a concert. I played until I was done. If people ask for an encore I don't go back. When your time is over, it's over. I think that the length of time of a concert and the length of time of the pieces are important. If the artist stays for the sake of staying on, he is making a mistake because he has to repeat himself. Therefore, he destroys what he did before. An artist must study himself , after all an artist is an actor.**

JM **Do you belong to the audience?**

BP **First of all I belong to the music, to myself and to the musicians who *play* with me.**

JM **In the end, the best way to respect the audience is to respect yourself...**

BP **Absolutely, the form, respect "*des planches*", it's very important. In America I understood that and I like to see an artist give the best of himself. Even if it's not possible you should not get below a certain level.**

JM **Does your great technique come from hard work?**

BP My teachers always said that I was technically very talented. I work on piano to perfect myself, but often I work without a piano. I do exercises in the air. Technique is the independence of the fingers, control of the relation between what you think and what you play. You get good technique by practicing a lot but mostly by thinking about the way you are going to play. I think a lot before I play. I don't want my fingers to command me. A great musician is like a great athlete, he must be physically strong and his mind must be well balanced. Then he'll do great things. That's the secret.

Article contributed by Arnie and Diana Fox.

Translation by Marc Kniebihler. Acquired from the Philadelphia Public Library. Exact date of interview and name of interviewer is unknown.

*Edits (**italicized**) Don Glanden 2006.*

Jessica Williams

From Wikipedia, the free encyclopedia

Jessica Williams is an American pianist who has deep roots in the Jazz Tradition and has a style that draws on Thelonius Monk, John Coltrane, and Miles Davis.

She was born in Baltimore, Maryland, on March 17, 1948. She was classically trained at the Peabody Conservatory of Music, beginning lessons at age seven.

She moved to Philadelphia during her teens and began playing with the great Philly Joe Jones, drummer for the Miles Davis Quintet.

She is a two-time Grammy nominee. In 1986, her album *Nothin' But The Truth* was nominated for a Grammy, and in late 2004, her album *LIVE at Yoshi's Volume One* was also nominated for a Grammy.

In her mid-twenties, she moved to California, where she played in the bands of Eddie Harris, Dexter Gordon, Tony Williams, Stan Getz, Big Nick Nicholaus, Airto and Flora, Charlie Rouse, John Abercrombie, Charlie Haden, Leroy

Vinnegar, and others.

She has released over 40 albums, including *Time to Burn on Red and Blue*(a trio w/Dave Captein, Mel Brown);*Some Ballads Some Blues on Red and Blue*(a trio w/Dave Captein, Mel Brown); *Jessica Plays for Lovers on Red and Blue*(solo piano); and *Live at Yoshi's Vol. One* and *Two on Maxjazz* (a trio w/Ray Drummond, Victor Lewis).

She received two grants from the National Endowment for the Arts (1984 and 1988); a Rockefeller Grant for composing (1989); the Alice B. Toklas Grant for Women Composers (1992), and the John Simon Guggenheim Memorial Foundation in 1995.

She has been presented the keys to the city of Sacremento, California, also receiving four grants from the Sacremento Arts Commission. She has also been presented the Keys to the City of San Mateo, California. In 2002 she was chosen Artist of the Year in Santa Cruz County, largely for her free musical service for elder members of the community, and donating support to the Women's Shelter of Watsonville, California. In Europe, she scored Jazz Record of the Year for 2 consecutive years in the Jazz Journal International Reader's Poll.

Still, she is better-known in Europe and Japan than in the USA.

She has produced more than 200 original compositions; and she has recorded for Jazz Focus, Candid, Concord,

Landmark-Fantasy, Timeless, Maxjazz, and her own company, Red and Blue Music. She also owns her own publishing company, JJW Music, and runs her own Internet CD mail-order business, jessicawilliams.com.

She appeared at the 2004 and 2006 Mary Lou Williams Women in Jazz Festivals at the John F. Kennedy Center for the Performing Arts in Washington, DC.

Sources

http://en.wikipedia.org/wiki/Jessica_Williams

jessicawilliams.com (http://www.jessicawilliams.com/introduction.html)

This page was last modified 05:07, 2 May 2006.

All text is available under the terms of the GNU Free Documentation License. (See Copyrights for details.) Wikipedia is a registered trademark of the Wikimedia Foundation Inc.

Discography Of Jessica Williams

1 Equinox on Red and Blue

2 Unity on Red and Blue

3 Standards, Vol. One on Red and Blue

4 Standards, Vol. Two on Red and Blue

5 Billy's Theme on Origin Arts

6 Steps on Red and Blue

7 Solo at the JBL Theatre on Red and Blue

8 Now!!! On Red and Blue

9 For Coltrane on Red and Blue

10 Time to Burn on Red and Blue

11 Some Ballads Some Blues on Red and Blue

12 Jessica Plays for Lovers on Red and Blue

13 Blue Tuesday on Red and Blue

14 Solo Compositions on Red and Blue

15 It's Jessica's Time on Red and Blue

16 As Time Goes By on Red and Blue

17 Offering on Red and Blue

18 More For Monk on Red and Blue

19 This Side Up on Maxjazz

20 All Alone on Maxjazz

21 Live at Yoshi's Vol.1 on Maxjazz

22 Live at Yoshi's Vol.2 on Maxjazz

23 Maybeck 2001 on Red and Blue

24 Millenial Meditations on Red and Blue

25 Without Walls on Red and Blue

26 Dedicated to You on Red and Blue

27 Song for Yusef on Red and Blue

28 Virtual Miles on Red and Blue

29 Impressions of Spain on Red and Blue

30 The Gift on Red and Blue

31 I Let a Song Go on Hep

32 The Next Step on Hep

33 The Real Deal on Hep

34 A Song That I Heard on Hep

35 In the Pocket on Hep

36 Blue Fire on Jazz Focus

37 Arrival on Jazz Focus

38 Encounters on Jazz Focus

39 Encounters II on Jazz Focus

40 Boss of the Bass on Jazz Focus

41 Victoria Concert on Jazz Focus

42 In the Key of Monk on Jazz Focus

43 Intuition on Jazz Focus

44 Inventions on Jazz Focus

45 Momentum on Jazz Focus

46 Joy on Jazz Focus

47 Gratitude on Candid

48 Heartland on Ear Art

49 Ain't Misbehavin' on Candid

50 Nothin' But the Truth on Blackhawk

51 Joyful Sorrow on Blackhawk

52 And Then There's This on Timeless

53 Jazz in the Afternoon on Candid

54 Higher Standards on Candid

55 Psi-Fi on Red and Blue

56 Jessica's Blues on Jazz Focus

57 Live in the UK on Red and Blue

58 Maybeck 1992 on Concord

59 Epistrophy w/Charlie Rouse on Fantasy
   Above all on CD's

60 The Portal of Antrim on Adelphi-Vinyl

61 **Rivers of Memory on Clean Cuts-Vinyl**

62 **Portraits (2 record set) on Adelphi-Vinyl**

63 **Update with Eddie Harris on Clean Cuts-Vinyl**

64 **Orgonomic Music on Clean Cuts-Vinyl**

Note: All CD's & Vinyl can be ordered directly from www.jessicawilliams.com.

Notes to Database

Explanation of abbreviations-Initials after the pianist name for the description of the CD or album is the name of the pianist. For example, Zumbrunn, Karen- K.Z.Trio is Karen Zumbrunn.

f-fusion, o-organ, pno.-piano, after description it is always an LP unless CD is written.

Any LP's listed may have been re-issued as a CD.

Date shown is either the date of performance or when the album was released. If there is no date, linear notes have omitted the date.

If the pianist is also a vocalist, it is listed if known.

Some of the artists listed may not be considered jazz pianists, but I have listed them if they have a jazz style. This is subject to interpretation.

Any artist that can be ordered from cdbaby.com, you can sample some of their songs from their website. Obviously, I did not listen to all the artists. If, there are any errors or omissions, please let me know so that I can correct them in future compendiums.

The description will list the Title of album or CD, date of performance or release date, record label, catalogue number, LP or CD.

All artists from cdbaby.com only list the Title of CD. All the detailed information can be gotten from their website, biography of artist, dates, etc.

An artist in the data base may not be the leader on the LP or CD but a side-man. There may be other albums or CD's in which the artist is the leader. This is your reference point, so that if he or she appeals to your taste, you can research that artist for other LP's or CD's that they released. Happy hunting!

Links to Important Web-Sites

www.jessicawilliams.com

www.bernardpeiffer.com

www.manegemusic.com

www.cdbaby.com

www.iaje.org

www.allaboutjazz.com

www.donglanden.com

www.mosaic.com

www.tomlord.com

www.downbeat.com

Abel	Shane	Visitor (cdbaby.com)
Abene	Mike	You must have been a Beautiful Baby(1984, Stash 249)
Abney	Don	Concerto for drums by Louis Bellson (Verve Cleff, MG[1] V-8016)
Abrams	Muhal Richard	f- Arrisong (1975, Trio-Whynot 7121)
Acea	Johnny (John Adriano)	CD's w. Joe Newman-Al Cohn (Fresh Sound)
Adams	Terry	Terrible (1/95, New World 80464)CD- Piano & Organ
Adams	Tom	Beautiful Love (2006, trax connection, AMG-001)CD-pianist & vocalist
Adrian	Alex	Dream Again (Terra Nova) CD
Afterffect		Midnight Summertime (cdbaby.com)
Aguiar	Aloisio	King of Hearts (cdbaby.com)
Ahead	Straight	City Cuts (cdbaby.com)
Aikawa	Yuka	All Beings In the Whole Universe (cdbaby.com)
Aiken	Barry	Balboa Park (cdbaby.com)
Airborne		Take Off (cdbaby.com)
Aire	Gerry	The Fur Elise Jam and More (cdbaby.com)
Akagi	Kei	The Magicians (Concord with Flora Purim & Airto Moreira)
Ake	David	In Between (cdbaby.com)
Akiyoshi	Toshiko	Finesse (5/78, Concord Jazz)

Albam	Manny	M.A. And His Jazz Greats Play Music From West Side Story(Decca,DL4517)
Albany	Joe	Birdland birds, Inner City
Albert	Carol	Love In Your Eyes (cdbaby.com)
Alberts	Don	D.A.Trio-Intuition (cdbaby.com)
Albulescu	Eugene	Reverie (cdbaby.com)
Aldrich	Ronnie	Emotions (London LP,SP-44310)
Aless	Tony	Long Island Suite (1955, Roost 2202)
Alexander	Charlie	Johnny & Baby Dodd:Blue Piano Stomp (1928, Vic. 21554)
Alexander	Monty	We've Only Just Begun (Dec.1, 1971, BASF-MPS, 25-103)
Alford	Jonathan	Tenaya (cdbaby.com)
Ali	Hassan Ibn	The Max Roach Trio Featuring The Legendary H.A. (1964, Atlantic 782273-2)
Ali	David	A Deeper Level (cdbaby.com)
Allen	Geri	In the Year of the Dragon (Mar.1989, Polygram 834428)
Allen	Sam	China Boy (1937, Bb 6941)
Allen	Steve	Steve Allen at the Roundtable (Forum, F-9014)
Alless	Tony	Cocktail Swing-Jack Sterling & His Quintet (Columbia Harmony-HL-7202)
Allison	Mose	I've been doin' some thinkin' (1968, Atlantic, SD-1511)
Allyson	Karrin	Azure-Te (1993, Concord CCD-4641) Vocalist, Pianist

Alperin	Mikhail	Wave Over Sorrow (7/89, ECM 1396) CD
Alpert	Pauline	Ragtime Piano Interpretations (Folkways RF 24)
Altheimer	Joshua	No record under his name-with Big Bill Broonzy & Sonny Boy Williamson
Altman	Laurie	For Now at Least (12/29/81, Progressive 7066)
Alvaro	Romero	Anime gemelle (1953, Fonit 7214)
Alves	Helio	H.A. and Cadence Trio-Yatrata (cdbaby.com)
Ambrose	Amanda	The Amazing Amanda Ambrose-Her Songs...Her Piano(1963, RCA-LSP-2742)
Ameen	Tom	Treasure The Gift (cdbaby.com)
Ammons	Albert	A.A,. (1936-39, Classics)
Amsallem	Franck	Out a Day (1990, OMD CD1532)
Anderson	Chris	CD's w. Charlie Parker (Savoy)
Andrews	Jimmy	Pseudonym for Frank Banta
Antognini	Ivo	I.A. Jazz Project- Inspiration (cdbaby.com)
Anz	Johnny	The Music of J.A.- Piano & Voice (cdbaby.com)
Applegate	Richard	Warriors (cdbaby.com)
Archibald	Becky	Searching (cdbaby.com)
Argyris	Phill	P.A. Quartet w/Stan Strickland & Phil Grenadier-Point of Departure(cdbaby.com)
Arisa		We Are Part of Nature (cdbaby.com)

Armstrong	Lil	Chicago And All That Jazz! (Oct.1961, Verve, V-8441)
Arnay	David	Blues ...And Then Some (cdbaby.com)
Arndt	Bernhard	Inside Insight (7/92-10/95, FMP Own 90005)CD
Arnesen	Dag	Movin' (1-2/94, Thurus TRCD 832) CD
Aronov	Ben	CD's w. Vache; Peplowski (Concord)
Arriale	Lynne	The Eyes Have It (1993, DMP)
Arvanitas	George	Psychicemotus-Yustef Lateef, Impulse
Asaro	Paul	Parlor Piano Solos (cdbaby.com)
Ash	Marvin	Classics in Jazz-piano stylists (12/13/49, Capitol H323) 10"LP
Ashby	Wenso	Midnit Walkin' (cdbaby.com)
Aspland	Robin	Alec & Dankworth Generation Big Band:Nebuc Hadezzar('93),Scott'sJazzHousee)CD
Assad	Clarice	Invitation (cdbaby.com)
Atherton	Dana	Open Blinds (cdbaby.com)
Atwell	Winifred	Winifred Atwell & her piano with Ted Heath-Black & White Magic, London
Auer	Pepsi	M.Kleim: Honeysuckle Rose (1964, Sup. 33561)
August	Jan	Jan August Plays Songs To Remember (Mercury LP,MG-20072)
Austin	Lovie	L. A. & Her Blue Serenaders (1924-26, Fountain) CD
Axen	Bent	Let's Keep the Message (1960, Debut 133)

Ayers, Jr.	Leon	Compilations (cdbaby.com)
Azimuth		Photographs (cdbaby.com)
Azouhouni		I Gotta Go (cdbaby.com)
Azzi	Christian	Frog I-More-Rag(2/3/48-OSW493-1-Patheco54-16028)67B-Franklin Mint Jazz
B	Danny	Midnight Dream (cdbaby.com)
B	Stanley	All For Love (cdbaby.com)
Baaska	Don	From Puerto Rico With Love (cdbaby.com)
Bachrach	Matt	Along For The Ride (cdbaby.com)
Badgley	Bob	Tranquiltiy (cdbaby.com)
Baerman	Noah	N.B.Trio: U-Turn (cdbaby.com)
Bailey	Judy	J.B.Solo (1977, Eureka 107)
Baker	Philip	It's For Real (cdbaby.com)
Bales	Burton	After Hours Piano (1949, GTJ 19)
Balke	Jon	Further (6/93, ECM 1517) CD
Ball	Ronnie	All About Ronnie (Savoy, 12075)
Ballantyne	Jon	Sky Dance (12/88, Justin Time JUST 30)CD
Ballen	Eddie	Nocturnal Affair (cdbaby.com)
Band	The Red Stripe	You Got What You Asked For (cdbaby.com)

Banks	Don	Cherokee (1950, Jazzart 48) Pianist & composer
Banks	D.B.	Charlestown a Piano Journey (cdbaby.com)
Banta	Frank	Ragtime Piano Interpretations: (Folkways RF 24)
Barab	Miriam	Education of a Lover (cdbaby.com)
Baranco	Wilbert	Everytime I Think of You /Baranco's Boogie (1946, Black & White 42)
Barber	Patricia	Companion (7/99, Blue Note/Premonition 522963-2)CD-Piano & Vocal
Barber	Bobby	The Spirit Is Willing (cdbaby.com)
Bargard	Rob	Better Times (12/92-12/93, Criss Cross CRISS 1086) CD
Bargy	Roy	Pianoflage (8/31/22, Victor 18969) Side 53A-Franklin Mint Jazz
Barker	Stan	S.B. & Digby Fairweather: Let's Duet (1984, Essex)
Barnes	Darrell	If I Could (cdbaby.com)
Barnes	Dre'	The Enchanted One (cdbaby.com)
Barrett	Sweet Emma	S.E.B. and her New Orleans Music (1963, SLND 241)
Barrett	Michael	Redemption (cdbaby.com)
Barron	Kenny	K.B. at Maybeck-Volume 10, Concord,CCD4466
Barta	Steve	Blue River (cdbaby.com)
Barth	Bruce David	Morning Call (7/94, Enja 8084)CD
Barton	Tim	Turnin' (cdbaby.com)

Basie	Count	Basie one more time (Roulette, R-52024)
Bassini	Piero	Lush Life (6/90, Splasc(h) H341-2) CD
Bateman	Charles	Three Swinging Bells (Herald 0100 with Aaron Bell)
Bates	Collin	Bruce Turner: ?
Bates	Django (Leon)	Delightful Precipice (1986, Loose Tubes 003)
Batiste	Jonathan	Times in New Orleans (cdbaby.com)
Battaglia	Stefano	Confession (3/91, Splasc(h) H 334-2)CD
Battat	Abe	Once Around the Block (TAPE)
Beach	Bill	Letting Go (cdbaby.com)
Beal	Charlie	Original Motion Picture Soundtrack:New Orleans(1946, Giants of Jazz 1025)
Beal	Eddie	Young Man's Blues -Claude Trenier (1946, Lamplighter 102)Piano & songwriter
Bean	Floyd	M. Spanier: Lazy Piano Man (1950, Mer. 5424)
Beard	Jim	Lost at the Carnival (1994, Lipstick LIP 89027) CD
Beatty	William	Song of Unconditional Love (cdbaby.com)
Beck	Gordon	The French Connection 2 (1982, JMS 018)
Beck	Pia	Pia's Boogie (1950, Phi. 34176H)
Becker	Marcus	Lacuna (6/91, LTR CDLR 45043) CD
Becker	John	Are You In A Band? (cdbaby.com)

Beckwith	Rickie Byars	Soul Fulfilling (cdbaby.com)
Bedell	Josh	Becuzuvu (cdbaby.com)
Beirach	Richie	R.B. at Maybeck-Volume 19, Concord,CCD4518
Bell	Graeme	Humphrey Littleton: Jazz at the Royal Festival Hall/Jazz at the Conway Hall '54 Dormouse) CD
Bello	Nathan	Rose City Rag (cdbaby.com)
Bennett	Don	Solar (8/94, Candid CACD 79723) CD
Bennett	Lou	o- The L.B. Quartet (1960, RCA 430050)
Bennett	Richard Rodney	Carol Sloane-Love You Madly (1988, Contemporary, C 14049)
Benoit	David	David Benoit-Waiting for Spring (1989, GRP, GR-9595)
Benskin	Sammy	Idaho (BN 514)
Beresford	Steve	Three Pianos (7/23/01, Emanem)
Berg	Shelly	Will: A Tribute to Oscar Peterson (March 25-26,1997, Cars)
Berger	Karl	Interludes (1977, FMP 0460) also vibraphonist & teacher
Bergman	Borah	A New Frontier (1/83, Soul Note 121030)CD
Berlin	Ben	You're the Cream in my Coffee (1929, Grammophon22401)Bandleader,arrang.
Berman	Ken	K.B. Trio (cdbaby.com)
Bermejo	Mili	A Time For Love (cdbaby.com)
Bernard	Mike	Ragtime Piano Interpretations: (Folkways RF 24)

Berner	Ernst	Tiger Rag (1936, Parl. B35513) Band called Berry's
Bernhardt	Warren	Bobby/Billy/Brasil-featuring voice of Luiz Henrique(Verve LP,V/V6-8723)
Bernstein	Elmer	Paris Swings (Capitol, T-1288)
Besiakov	Ben	You Stepped Out of a Dream (3/90, Steeplechase SCCD-31265)CD
Betz	Alfy	Alfy Betz with The Salt Lake Bad Boys (cdbaby.com)
Bey	Taslimah	T.B.-Live! (cdbaby.com)
Bicnase	David	Dreams (cdbaby.com)
Bietry	Brad	The B.B. Jazz Group-Skylark (cdbaby.com)
Bigger	Laraine	Loose Change (cdbaby.com)
Bilowus	David	David,Sarah, and Andrew Bilowus-Year of the Cicada (cdbaby.com)
Binder	Aaron	Bang the Drum Quickly (cdbaby.com)
Birnbaum	Mark	Hot Piano! Ragtime Blues Jazz Classical M.B. (cdbaby.com)
Bishop	Walter Jr.	Walter Bishop, Jr.-Soliloquy (Jan.1975, Seabreeze, SB-1002)
Bjornstad	Ketil	The Sea (9/94, ECM 1545) CD
Blake	Eubie	The Eighty-six Years of E.B. (1969, Col. C2S847)
Blake	Ran	f- Third Stream Recompositions (1977, Owl 017)
Blake	Dick	How Deep Is The Ocean (cdbaby.com)
Blatter	Al	A.B.Trio:Dumont 18 (cdbaby.com)

Bley	Carla	f- Escalator over the Hill (1968-71, JCOA EOTH)
Bley	Paul	f- Tango Palace (1983, SN 1090)
Bloom	Rube	Soliloquoy (1927, OK 40867) Pianist & composer
Bloom	Mark	Brooklyn Roots (cdbaby.com)
Blount	Herman "Sonny"	See Sun Ra
Bluestein	Michael	Ambient Soul (cdbaby.com)
Bluth	Larry	Formations (10/96-2/98, Zinnia 114)CD
Blythe	Jimmy	In Chronological Order (1924-31, Document)
Boatman	Armand	Armand Boatman-Live at Gregory's (1984, PAUSA, PR-7166)
Bob	Black	Big Bill Bronzy-Pneumonia Blues, Big Bill Blues, Matchbook Blues(1936)
Bohler	Fred	China Boy (1941, Col. ZZ1020) also bandleader
Boland	Francy	Chet Baker in Paris Volume 3(12/55-3/56, Emarcy 837476)-2CD
Boland, Jr.	Clay	Love Walked In (cdbaby.com)
Bolling	Claude	C.B. With The Help Of My Friends (1975, Who's Who In Jazz, WW21018)
Bommarito	Charlie	Moments of Grace (cdbaby.com)
Bonafede	Salvatore	CD's w. Enzo Randisi (Splasch)
Bonfils	Kjeld	Morrocco (1943, Odeon D900)
Bonnemere	Eddie	Piano Bons-Bons By Bonnemere (Roost, 2236)LP

Bonner	Joe	Devotion (1983, Ste. 1182)
Bonnier	Bess	Xmazz (1993, Jack Brokensh Quartet, AEM)
Booker	Beryl	Billy Holiday: Lady Love (1954, UA 5014)
Borthwick	Ramona	A New Leaf (cdbaby.com)
Bostwick	Nan	N.B. & Tom Brier: Dualing at the McCoys(both pianists) (cdbaby.com)
Bottlang	Rene	Round About Bobby (10/92, Planisphare PL 1267-9) CD
Boudin	Morgan	It's A Mystery To Me (cdbaby.com)
Boulevard	Glassbrick	A Simple Dream (cdbaby.com)
Bowin	Maurice	Romantic Jazz Standards (cdbaby.com)
Bowman	Dave	Cow Cow Boogie/Stars Fell on Alabama(1946, Sig.28126)
Bown	Patty	Patty Bown Plays Big Piano, Columbia
Boxer	Karl	The Karl Boxer Trio-Split Decision, Dot
Boyd	Eddie	Third Degree (1951-59, Charly BM042)
Brackeen	Joanne	AFT (12/77, Timeless SJP 115)CD
Bradshaw	Evans	Pieces of Eighty-Eight-Evans Bradshaw Trio (Jan.1959, Riverside, RLI-12-296)
Braga	Leandro	E Por Que Nao?(And Why Not?) (1991, Arabesque Jazz AJ 104)
Brancato	Ted	Jeanie Bryson-Tonight I Need You So (1994, Telarc CD-83348)CD
Brand	Dollar	See Abdullah Ibrahim

Brannon	Teddy	CD's w. Don Byas (Savoy)
Bravo	Sonny	Tito Puente and his Latin Ensemble-Mambo-Diablo (1985, Concord, CJP-283)
Breckenridge	Dardanelle	Jazz Women- A Feminist Retrospective, Stash
Bredin	Ron	Boogie Improv (cdbaby.com)
Brenders	Stan	1942-accompanied Django Reinhardt
Brennan	John Wolf	Henceforward (5/88, Core COCD 900871 0)CD
Bright	Ronnell	Bright's Spot (1956, Reg. 6041)Pianist & composer
Bril	Igor	Pered Zakhodom Solnta(1985. Twilight, Mel. C6021873003)Composer
Brink	Bert VanDen	Chet Baker: Hazy Hugs (9/85, Limetree MLP 198601)
Brinson	Cy	Cy by Night (cdbaby.com)
Britt	Dale	Rhonda Apple & The D.B.Trio: Rising Tide (cdbaby.com)
Britto	Carol	Alone Together (1980's, Town Crier Records)
Broadbent	Alan	A.B. at Maybeck-Volume 14, Concord,CCD4488
Brock	Herbie	Solo-Herbie Brock at the Piano (Savoy, MG-12066)
Brooks	Hadda	Women in Jazz- Pianists, Stash
Brooks	Harvey	Stuff (1930, Vic.38122) Pianist & composer
Brothers	Two	Julio Figueroa & Thiago Pinheiro- Live at Canal 52 (cdbaby.com)
Broussard	Al	The Music Of A Lifetime (cdbaby.com)

Brown	Charles	Charles Brown-One More For The Road (Alligator, AL-4771)LP
Brown	Cleo	Boogie Woogie (1935, Decca 477)
Brown	Donald	Sources of Inspiration (Aug.11, 1989. Muse 5385)
Brown	Vernell Jr.	A Total Eclipse
Brown	Doug	Shades of Brown (cdbaby.com)
Brown	Peter	Marie-Claude (cdbaby.com)
Brown	Roy	Jazz is the Music I Play (cdbaby.com)
Brown	Jonathan	Shades of Brown (cdbaby.com)
Brownlow	Jack	J.B.Trio -Suddenly It's Bruno (JFCD 031) Jazz Focus
Brubeck	Dave	Jazz:Red Hot And Cool-The Dave Brubeck Quartet (Columbia, CL-699)
Bruder	Rudy	Rudy's Boogie (1946, Victory 9009)
Brueggemann	Eli	Launchpad (cdbaby.com)
Bruninghaus	Rainer	Continuum (9/83, ECM 1266)
Brunotte	Gary	Yesterday's Dream (cdbaby.com)
Bryant	Gary Paul	Imaginary Piano (cdbaby.com)
Bryant	Ray	Ray Bryant-Me And The Blues (1957-58, Prestige 2LP's, P-24038)
Buchman	Bill	The B.B.Trio-Out of the Blue (cdbaby.com)
Buckner	Milt	M.B., Jo Jones,Slam Stewart-Jazz Greatest Names, Black & Blue

Buckner	Steve	Darkness Into Light Vol.1-Deep Meditation (cdbaby.com)
Budwig	Arlette McCoy	I Still Love You (cdbaby.com)
Buie	Reggie	The R.B. Trio- The First Time (cdbaby.com)
Bunch	John	The Great New Gene Krupa Quartet Featuring C.Ventura ('64, Verve, V6-8584)
Bunink	Nico	Tell Me (1979, Jimmy Knepper, Daybreak 001)
Burch(ell)	John	Don Rendell: Roarin' (1961, JLND 951)
Burk	Greg	G.B.Trio-Nothing, Knowing (cdbaby.com)
Burns	Ralph	Very Warm For Jazz (1958, Decca 9207)Arranger, composer, pianist
Burrell	Dave	f- Windward Passages (1979, HH 5)
Burrell	Duke	Louisiana Shakers Band (1974, Crescent Jazz 3)
Burson	Claudia	My Foolish Heart (cdbaby.com)
Burton	Rahn	Bright Moments (1973, Atl. 2-907)
Burton	Buddy	Chicago Southside:Blues & Jazz 1928-36(Feb.1928-Apr.2,1936, RST)
Busch	Lou	Lazy Rhapsody-Lou Busch his piano and orchestra (Capitol, T-1072)
Bushkin	Joe	Joe Bushkin Turns Doctor Dolittle On (Columbia, CS-9615)
Busiakiewicz	Richard	The Ray Gelato Giants Live in Italy (1999, Double Scoop Records)CD
Butler	Henry	For all Seasons (6/95, Atlantic 82856-2) CD
Butler	Bett	Short Stories (cdbaby.com)

Byard	Jaki	J.B. at Maybeck-Volume 17, Concord,CCD4511
Byrd	Eric	The Eric Byrd Trio (cdbaby.com)
C To C		Less Is More (cdbaby.com)
Cables	George	Cables Vision (1979, Cont. 14001)
Cain	Mike	Strange Omen (11/90, Candid CCD 79505)CD
Caine	Uri	Ruth Naomi Floyd: Paradigms for Desolate Times (Contour Records)
Calderazzo	Joey	To Know One (1991, Blue Note CDP 7981652)CD
Caldwell	Maurice	All About Me (cdbaby.com)
Caldwell	George O.	CD's w. Carmen Bradford (Amazing)
Call	Bob	House Party Groove by "Nature Boy"Brown(around 1950,United Label)
Cameron	Bruce	With All My Love (cdbaby.com)
Camilo	Michel	Michel Camilo (Jan. 3, 1988-Feb.1, 1988, Portrait)
Camp	Red	Red Camp Inventions (Cook, 1087)
Campbell	John	J.C. at Maybeck-Volume 29, Concord,CCD4581
Cannon	Lynn	Working It! (cdbaby.com)
Cano	Eddie	Here is the Fabulous E.C. (1961, Reprise R6055)
Capers	Valerie	Affirmation (1982, KMA Arts)
Cappelletti	Arrigo	Singolari Equilibri (4/92- Splasc(h) H 390-2) CD

Cardall	Paul	Miracles-A Journey of Hope & Healing (cdbaby.com)
Cardillo	Bobby	Bobby and Harry Cardillo: The Best Thing For You(would be us) (cdbaby.com)
Carey	Dave	The Dave Carey Quintet-Bandwagon Plus 2 (Laurie, LLP1004)LP
Carlberg	Frank	Steve Grover Consideration (IM-2011) CD
Carle	Frankie	Frank Carle plays the Great Piano Hits (1965, RCA, LSP-3425)
Carlisle	Una Mae	singer- Mean to me (1938, Voc. 198)
Carlson	Dave	Relax! ... with Dave Carlson (Hifirecord, R-203)
Carlson	Geoffrey	Invitation by Les Brown & His Band of Renown(Coral 10" LP, CRL-56108)
Carmichael	Judy	Jazz Piano (Jun.11, 1983, Statiras 8074)
Carmichael	Hoagy	Hoagy Carmichael-A Legendary Performer & Composer (RCA, CPL1-3370)
Carpenter	Ike	Sleepy Time Gal/Sleepy Time Down South('52, Intro 7504)Pir
Carr	Joe "Fingers"	J.F.C. Goes Continental (Capitol T1000)
Carr	Leroy	Big Four Blues, Going Back Home, Six Cold Feet in the Ground('35)singer,pno.
Carr	Mike	o. Live at Ronnie Scott's (1979, Spot. 517)
Carr	Robert	Finer Moments (cdbaby.com)
Carroll	Barbara	Have You Met Miss Carroll? (RCA, LPM-1137)
Carrus	Paolo	Sardegna Oltre II Mare (7/90-1/92, Splasc(h) CDH 373-2) CD
Carson	Tee	T.C.Trio at the Cypress Club (cdbaby.com)

Carter	Daniel	D.C.,William Parker,Federico Ughi:The Dream (cdbaby.com)
Carter	Steve	Jazmine (cdbaby.com)
Cary	Dick	D.C. (1957, Golden Crest 3024) Pianist,alto horn,trumpeter,arranger
Cary	Marc.	Abraham Burton: Closest to the Sun (1994, Enja ENJ - 8047)
Caselli	Alexandra	Out of the Aquarium (cdbaby.com)
Cashwell	Brian	Pure Imagination (cdbaby.com)
Castle	Geoff	e Expanded (1994, Turret)
Castro	Arturo	Latin & Hip-The Brothers Castro (Capitol LP,T-1706)arranger,vocalist & pianist
Castro	Joe	Mood Jazz-Joe Castro with voices & strings (Atlantic, 1264)
Catney	Dave	Jade Visions(1991, Justice)
Cavallaro	Carmen	Carmen Cavallaro Plays His Show Stoppers (Decca, DL-4018)
Cavanaugh	Page	Something's Happening at Page Cavanaugh's (Reprise, R-6053)
Caviani	Laura	Going There (cdbaby.com)
Celletti	Alessandra	Scott Joplin's Ragtime (cdbaby.com)
Chaix	Henri	Jumpin' Punkins (10/90, Sackville CD2-2020)CD
Chakmakian	Armen	Caravans (cdbaby.com)
Chandler	Chris	88 Keys & The Swing Kats (cdbaby.com)
Chaney	Ken	Xperience:Paradise (cdbaby.com)

Charette	Brian	B.C.Trio: Live at Deanna's (cdbaby.com)
Charlap	Bill	CD's w. Marvin Stamm (Music Masters)
Charles	Marvin	Melodies From The Heart (cdbaby.com)
Charles	Ray	Volume One-The Ray Charles Story (Atlantic, 8063)
Chase	The	The Chase: Clearly the Good Life! (cdbaby.com)
Cheatham	Jeannie	Blues and Boogie Masters (1993, Concord)
Cherif	Wajdi	Jasmine (cdbaby.com)
Cherner	Jarrett	J.C.Trio-Burgeoning (cdbaby.com)
Chesky	David	Rush Hour (1979, Columbia)LP
Chestnut	Cyrus	C.C. Revelation (Jun.7 &8, 1993, Atlantic)
Chevallier	Christian	French Toast (Angel 60009) Pianist & Arranger
Childs	Billy	Take For Example This (1988, Hip Pocket)
Ching	Larry	Till the End of Time (cdbaby.com)
Chittison	Herman	Cocktail Time-Herman Chittison Trio-Soft Winds (Royale 10" LP, 1824)
Chizhik	Leonid	Reministsentsii (1980, MEL. C60161558)
Chnee	Sergio Igor	Brazillian Contemporary Piano (cdbaby.com)
Choi	Janny	Ecstasy (cdbaby.com)
Christian	Jodie	Experience (1991-92, Delmark DD454)

Christopher		With and Without Words (cdbaby.com)
Ciacca	Antonio	Hollis Avenue (1/99, YVP 3075)CD
Cicero	Eugen	My Lyrics: E.C. in Tokyo (1977, Denon YX751OND)
Cion	Sarah	To You (Israeli label with Shlomo Goldenberg) CD
Cipelli	Roberto	Moona Moore (11-12/88, Splasc(h) H 173)
Cirillo	Wally	W.C. Quartet (1955, Savoy 15055)
Clare	Alan	Jazz Around The Clock (1958, Decca LK4260)
Clark	Curtis	Deep Sea River (3/85, Nimbus NS 3580)
Clark	Garnet	Piano & Swing (1935-8, Pathe) also feat. Teddy Weatherford & Garland Wilson
Clark	Gus	Appel de la jungle/ Paradise negre (1944, HOT 20)
Clark	Sonny	Dial S for Sonny (1957, BN 1570)
Clark	Matt	Paging Miss Love (cdbaby.com)
Clausen	Thomas	Piano Music (1989, M. A. Music A 801)CD
Claxton	Rozelle	Chicago: The Living Legends (1961, Riv. 9406)Pianist & arranger
Clement	Dawn	Hush (cdbaby.com)
Clemons	Joel	J.C. & The Lemons-Fresh Squeezed (cdbaby.com)
Close	Michael	I'm By Myself (cdbaby.com)
Coates	John Jr.	After the Before-John Coates, Jr. (Omnisound, N-1021)

Cochrane	Michael	Elements (9/85, Soul Note SN 1151)
Cockrell	Marvin F.	Heat (cdbaby.com)
Cody	Chris	Oasis (4/98, Naxos Jazz 860188-2)CD
Coggins	Gil	Ray Draper with John Coltrane (1957, NJ 8228)
Cohen	Adrian	The A.C.Trio: Standardized (cdbaby.com)
Cohen	David Bennett	In The Pocket (cdbaby.com)
Cohn	Zinky	Golden Lily Blues (1930, MLT. 12009)
Coker	Charles	The Incredible John Collins feat. Harry "Sweets" Edison('82,84,Nilva,NQ3412)
Coker	Dolo	All Alone (1978, Xan. 178)
Cole	Bobby	New!New! New!-The Bobby Cole Trio (Columbia, CL 1536)
Cole	Freddy	I'm Not My Brother, I'm Me (4/90, Sunnyside SSC 1054) CD
Cole	Buddy	Buddy Cole Plays Cole Porter (1958, Warner Bros., WS-1226)
Cole	Nat 'King'	Penthouse Serenade-Nat 'King' Cole at the piano (Capitol, T-332)
Coleman	Cecelia	Words of Wisdom (1993, L.A.P.)CD
Coleman	Gloria	o-Nat Simpkin Album-Piano
Coleman	Anthony	Sephardic Tinge (1993 & 1994, Tzadik)
Coleman	Marcus	Marcus Coleman (cdbaby.com)
Coleman	Cy	Cool Coleman (Westminster, WST-1500)

Colen	Pam	Pam Colen & Slomka-Pam 2 (cdbaby.com)
Colianni	John	John Colianni (8/86, Concord Jazz CCD 4309)CD
Collett	Frank	Terry Gibbs/Buddy DeFranco:Jazz Party-First Time Together(Palo Alto)
Colligan	George	Stomping Ground (9/97, Steeplechase SCCD 31441)CD
Collins	Joyce	A Fusion of Ellington and Gershwin (1982)
Collins	Ann	A.C.Trio:6:05 Central Standard Time (cdbaby.com)
Colombo	Massimo	Alexander (1-2/89, Splasc(h) H 177)
Coltrane	Alice	Transfiguration (1978, WB 3218)
Conington	Adrian	Solsonata (cdbaby.com)
Connell	Michael	Country Aire (cdbaby.com)
Connick,Jr.	Harry	We Are in Love (1990, Columbia 46146)
Conroy	Jim	The Edd & I (cdbaby.com)
Conte	Al	Mr. Piano & Mr. Banjo-Al Conte Quartet (VIP-2001)
Coogan	Chris	Jazz by Coogan (cdbaby.com)
Cook	Doc	Alligator Crawl/Brainstorm (1927, Col. 1298D)Pianist & arranger
Cook	Gerald	Libby Holman: The Ballads & Blues (Evergreen MR 6501)
Cook	David	Green (cdbaby.com)
Copeland	Eric	Stolen Moments (cdbaby.com)

Copland	Marc.	My Foolish Heart (Jazz City) played Sax as Marc Cohen
Corea	Chick	Chick Corea and return to forever-light as a feather (1973, Polydor, PD-5525)
Cornford	Bob	Tony Coe: Tournee Du Chat (1981-2, Nato)
Correll	Rob	It's Groovy Baby (cdbaby.com)
Cortopassi	David	Embrace Destiny (cdbaby.com)
Corwin	Bob	Chet Baker Plays the Best of Lerner & Loewe(7/59, OJC 137) CD
Costa	Eddie	The Eddie Costa-Vinnie Burke Trio (Jubilee, JGM-1025)
Costa	Johnny	Johnny Costa Piano Solos (Coral, CRL-57020)
Costa Da	Raie	Ragtime Piano Interpretations (Folkways RF 24)
Cottonwood	Bobby	Smile (cdbaby.com)
Covey	Susan	Where Evening Becomes Night (cdbaby.com)
Cowell	Stanley	S.C. at Maybeck-Volume 5, Concord,CCD4431
Cox	Paul	P.C.Project (cdbaby.com)
Craft	Bob	My Life: In Search Of The Dance (cdbaby.com)
Crane	Fred	The Al Belleto Sextette-Half And Half (Capitol, T-751)
Cray	Dan	Dan Cray Trio-Save Us (cdbaby.com)
Crews	Freddie	The Famous Castle Jazz Band-The Five Pennies, Contemporary
Criner	Clyde	Behind The Sun (10/87, RCA Novus PL 83029)CD

Crispell	Marilyn	A Concert in Berlin (Jul.2, 1983, Free Music 46)
Crosara	Francesco	Colors (cdbaby.com)
Crothers	Connie	Concert At Cooper Union (1/84, New Artists NA 1002)CD
Crump	Jesse	Bear-Mash Blues (1923, Para. 12087) Pianist & organist
Cuevas	Carlos	Depiction (cdbaby.com)
Cunimondo	Frank	Totally Frank (cdbaby.com)
Cunliffe	Bill	Satisfaction (cdbaby.com)
Curiosity		The Forced Magician (cdbaby.com)
Curley	Patrick	3's A Crowd:Inspirations (cdbaby.com)
Curtis	Barbara	Solos and Duets (1993, Sackville)CD-Barbara Sutton Curtis
Cushnine	Scott	S.C.,Doug Riley,Tyler Yarema & L. Anderson:Two Pianos, No Wait. (cdbaby.com)
Cuypers	Leo	Zeeland Suite & Johnny Rep Suite (9/74-9/77, Buhanst 9307)CD
D	Barry	Handprint (cdbaby.com)
Dagari		Crossing the Sahels (cdbaby.com)
Dagmar	Anna	Solo Songs (cdbaby.com)
Dahl	Carsten	Message From Bud (12/98, Storyville STCD 4232)CD
Dahl	Caroline	Night House (cdbaby.com)
Dailey	Albert	Buddy DeFranco-Mr. Lucky, Pablo

Dallwitz	Dave	(Swaggie) Pianist, Composer, Leader-Ragtime
Dalton	Bert	Midnight Coffee (cdbaby.com)
D'Ambrosio	Meredith	Another Time (Sunnyside SSC 1017D)CD
Dameron	Tadd	The Magic Touch (1962, Riv. 9419)
D'Andrea	Franco	Dialogues With Superego (3/80, Red 123157)
Dandridge	Putney	When I Grow Too Old To Dream (1935, Voc.2982)Pianist & Singer
Danielsson	Per	Dream Dancing (cdbaby.com)
Danko	Harold	Chet Baker: Once Upon a Summertime(2/77, OJC 405)CD
D'Anna	Sandy	Full Throttle (cdbaby.com)
Dapogny	Jim	Sippie Wallace: Sippie (1982, Atl. 19350)
Dardanelle		See Dardanelle Breckenridge or Dardanelle Hadley?
Darling	Floyd	Chet Baker: My Foolish Heart (IRD TDM 002)CD
Dauner	Wolfgang	e- Solo Piano (1981, Mood 28635)
Davenport	Cow Cow	Cow Cow Blues/State Street Drive (CI)(VO 1198)-Boogie Woogie
David	Rus	Echoes Of Harlem (Decca 10",DL5369)
David	Ronnie	In The Still Of The Night (cdbaby.com)
Davidson	Lowell	L.D. Trio (1965, ESP-Disk ESP 1012-2)
Davies	Lyndon	In My Dreams (cdbaby.com)

Davis	Copeland	Endangered Species (cdbaby.com)
Davis	Anthony	f- Past Lives (1978, Red 134)
Davis	Blind John	B.J. Davis (Apr.-Nov. 1938, Story of the Blues 3520)
Davis	Walter (,Jr.)	Four Hundred Years Ago Tomorrow (1979, Owl 020)
Davis	Wild Bill	o- Impulsions (1972, BB 33037)
Davis	Ron	Solo Duo Trip (cdbaby.com)
Davis	Suzzanne	S.D. Quartet- Hymn To Freedom (cdbaby.com)
Davis	Bamm	Short Stories (cdbaby.com)
Davis	Stan	CV's Mood (cdbaby.com)
Davis	Neil	Blue Moment (cdbaby.com)
Davis	John T.	Last of the Blues (cdbaby.com)
Dawson	Christopher	Introducing C.D. (cdbaby.com)
Dawson		Dawson's New Rage (cdbaby.com)
Dayce	Ernest	Heaven (cdbaby.com)
Dean	Roger	The Next Room (1992, Tall Poppies) Piano, Synthesizer
Dearie	Blossom	Once Upon A Summertime-Blossom Dearie (Verve, MGV-2111)
Dearing	Tamara	Yesterconfessions (cdbaby.com)
Decou	Walter	Panama (6/11/42-MLB140:JazzMan 8)Side 67B- Franklin Mint Jazz

Dee	Brian	Homeing In (5/88-2/89, Spotlite SPJ539)CD
Deems		L. A. Live (cdbaby.com)
DeFrancesco	Joey	o- Reboppin' (1992, Columbia 48624)
Degen	Bob	Sequoia Song (1976, Enja 2071)
DeGraaff	Rein De	Cloud People (1983, Timeless 191)
Degreg	Phil	Table For Three (cdbaby.com)
DeGregori	Rio	At the Woodchoppers' Ball (1942, Col. ZZ1108)
Delaney	Peg	P.D.Trio:If I Had You (cdbaby.com)
Delano	Peter	Bite of the Apple (1994, Verve 521869-2)
Delbecq	Benoit	Pursuit (May 17-19, 1999, Songlines)
Dembski	Peter	Aura (cdbaby.com)
Deneau	Jan	J.D.& Friends- An Evening At Pebble (cdbaby.com)
Deneff	Peter	P.D. & Vik Momjian- Excursion (cdbaby.com)
Dennerlein	Barbara	o- Hot Stuff (6/90, Enja 6050)CD
Dennis	John	Debut Rarities Vol.5 New Piano Expressions('94, Fantasy/Orig. Jazz Classics)
Dennis	Matt	M.D. Plays and Sings (1957, Kapp 1024)
Derado	Tino	Trio (cdbaby.com)
Derenzo	Joe	Of Night And Day (cdbaby.com)

Des Plantes	Ted	Midnight Stomp (3-4/91, Stomp Off CD 1231) CD
Desmarais	Lorraine	L.D. Trio (Jazzimage, JZ 100)
DeWilde	Laurent	Off The Boat (1987, IDA 015)CD
Diachun	Melody	Lullaby of the Leaves (cdbaby.com)
Dial	Gary	Dial And Oatts (9-10/88, DMP 465)CD
Dibaudo	Bobby	So Nice To Come Home To (cdbaby.com)
Dibke	Boel	Sweet Fulfillment (1994, New Artists)
Dickerson	Dwight	Sooner or Later (1978, Dis. 792)
Dickie	Neville	The Robin's Return (1969, Major Minor)
Diekemper	Ralph	Solo Improvisation (cdbaby.com)
Diggs	David	Jazzwerk (cdbaby.com)
Dillon	Monica	All I Have Is A Moment (cdbaby.com)
DiMartino	John	Birds of the Heart (cdbaby.com)
Dinkelbach	Joe	Red Pepper (cdbaby.com)
Dinoto	Ronnie	Arenal (cdbaby.com)
DiNovi	Gene	My Funny Valentine (1985, Pedimega 2)with Ruby Braff
DiSabatino	Paolo	Threeo (cdbaby.com)
Discenza	Don	Free As A Bird (cdbaby.com)

Disley	Terry	Experience (cdbaby.com)
Dobbins	Bill	Dedications-Bill Dobbins (1981, Omnisound Jazz, N-1036)LP
Dockery	Sam	Evans (4/8/57-H4JB3342-Vik LXA 1115)Side 74A-Franklin Mint Jazz
Dodge	Larry	From A Quiet Place (cdbaby.com)
Dogan	Bob	Rings (cdbaby.com)
Doggett	Bill	o- Lionel Hampton presents B.D. (1977, Who's who in Jazz 21002)
Doky	Christian	Letters (2 & 4/91, Storyville STCD 4177)CD
Doky	Niels Lan	Close Encounter (7/89, Storyville SLP/STCD 4173)CD
Domancich	Sophia	L'Annees Des Treize Lunes (12/94, Seventh A XV)CD
Donaldson	John	Meeting in Brooklyn (9/93, Babel BDV 9405) CD
Donati	William	The European Touch featuring William Donati (Tampa, TP-17)
Donegan	Dorothy	It Happened One Night, Forum
Donelian	Armen	Secrets (2/88, Sunnyside SSC 1031)CD
Dorough	Bob	M.Davis: Sorcerer (1962, 1967 Col. GS9532)Pianist, singer, songwriter
Dorsey	Claude	What A Wonderful World (cdbaby.com)
Dowling	Benjamin	Ahimsa (cdbaby.com)
Downes	Wayne	The Buddy Tate Quartet (Sackville, 3027)LP
Downing	Johnny	An Evening At Johnny's (cdbaby.com)

Doyle	Elizabeth	E.D.(cdbaby.com)
Dozier	Paulette	With You (cdbaby.com)
Drane	Arizona	Women in Jazz- Pianists, Stash
Dreamclassics	The	Reflections (cdbaby.com)
Drew	Jimmy	Indigo-J.D. (Decca, DL 74235) Vocal
Drew	Kenny Jr.	Third Phase (6/89, Jazz City 660 53 002)CD
Drew	Kenny	Kenny Drew-Solo Piano-Everything I Love (1976, Inner City, IC-2007)
Drinkard	Carl	The Complete Billy Holiday on Verve (1/23/54) CD2
Duchin	Eddie	Dream Along Eddy Duchin at the piano (Columbia, CL-1432)
Duchin	Peter	Invitation-Peter Duchin-his Piano and Strings (Decca, DL-74471)
Dudley	Bruce	Semblance (cdbaby.com)
Duke	Royce	Music in Black & White Vol.2 (cdbaby.com)
Duke	George	The 1976 Solo Keyboard Album (1976, Epic 32808)
Dulin	Michael	Atmospheres (cdbaby.com)
Duncan	Henry	Maple Leaf Rag/ I Give you my Word (1944, Black & White 31)
Dundas	Chris	C.D.Group (cdbaby.com)
Dunham	Keith	Master Jazz Piano- Vol.1 &2 (MJR)
Dunlap	Donnie	Donnie Dunlap & Piano...My Old Strawberry Hat(D.Dunlap Production,H-155)

Dupont	Jules	a.k.a. Andre Persiany
Dupree	Champion Jack	Jazz Piano Volume 9(Folkways FJ 2809)
Dupuis	Catherine	Moments (cdbaby.com)
Duquesnel	Peggy	Where is Love? (cdbaby.com)
Dybka	Darryl	Curiosity Dance (cdbaby.com)
Dzubinski	David	Recyclical (cdbaby.com)
Eames	Rich	Upstream/Downstream (cdbaby.com)
Eanet	Larry	Piano Solos Vol.1 (11/97, Jump JCD 12-20)CD
Earland	Charles	o- Leaving This Planet (Dec.11-13, 1973, Fantasy 66002)
Eaton	Steve	Home for Christmas (cdbaby.com)
Eaton	Johnny	Far Out, Near In-Johnny Eaton and his Princetonians (Columbia, CL-996)
Eaves	Hubert	I've Known Rivers and Other Bodies (1973, Prst. 66001)
Eckoff	Burt	Ecology (cdbaby.com)
Eckroth	Rachel	Mind (cdbaby.com)
Eckstein	Willie	Ragtime Interpretations (Folkways RF 24)
Eddins	William	Bad Boys , Vol.1 (cdbaby.com)
Edge	Katahdin's	The Ridge (cdbaby.com)
Edwards	Chad	Resolution (cdbaby.com)

Eicher	Alan	Pyramids (cdbaby.com)
Eldar		Eldar (2004, Sony Classical)CD
Eldridge	Rick	Solo Flights (cdbaby.com)
Eli		My Own Stuff (cdbaby.com)
Elias	Eliane	Plays Jobim (12/89, Blue Note CDP 7030892)CD
Eliez	Thierry	Dee Dee Bridgewater: Keeping Tradition (1992, Verve 519607-2)
Elizalde	Fred	Jazz at the Savoy: The 20's (1927-8, Decca) Piano, Composer, Leader
Elkjer	Robert	Clean Lines (cdbaby.com)
Ellington	Duke	The Symphonic Ellington-500 of Europe's finest musicians (Reprise, R-6097)
Elliott	Hiram	Paradise Hotel (cdbaby.com)
Elliott	Terence	The Professor: The New Jazz Swing (cdbaby.com)
Elliott	Byron J.	B.J.E. Presents "Keys to Christmas" (cdbaby.com)
Elmer	Steve	CD's w. Jazz Mentality (Vai) also plays drums
Emborg	Jorgen	(1979, No.2, 1983 Stunt 8302) Pianist, leader, composer
Emmanuele	Giuseppe	A Waltz For Debby (1/90, Splasc(h) H 200)CD
Enriquez	Bobby	The Wild Man-Prodigious Piano, GNP
Ensemble	Rochford Jazz	Roch4D (cdbaby.com)
Entmacher	Ed	The Gaze of Love (cdbaby.com)

Erickson	John	And So On (cdbaby.com)
Ernst	Charlie	Paraiso-Jazz Brazil (1993, Telarc-G.Mulligan with J.Duboc,CD83361)
Espinosa	Damian	D.E.Trio- The End of the New (cdbaby.com)
ESQ		Dizzy (cdbaby.com)
Evans	Gil	The Individualism Of Gil Evans (9/63, 4 & 7/84, Verve 833804)CD
Evans	John	Mainstream Jazz Piano(Omega, OSL-49)
Evans	Orrin	Grown Folk Bizness (Criss 1175) CD
Evans	Buck	Nize Baby (cdbaby.com)
Evans	Candace	So Nice (cdbaby.com)
Evans	Bill	Bill Evans-Affinity (1978, Warner Bros., BSK-3293)
Evans	Lee	Piano Plus-Lee Evans (Capitol, T-1708)
Evens	Gabe	G.E.Trio-Connection (cdbaby.com)
Ewell	Don	Don Ewell (Chiaroscuro, Sept.25, 1973-1974)
Excitement	Mr.	Big Mamma & Mr.Excitement: B.M.Sue & Mr.Excitement (cdbaby.com)
Fair	Jane	J.F./Rosemary Galloway Quintet: Waltz Out (cdbaby.com)
Fallon	Ray	George Adams: Old Feeling (3/11-12, 1991, Blue Note 96689) CD
Farao	Massimo	For Me (12/90, Splasc(h) H 337-2)CD
Farnham	Allen	At Maybeck Recital Hall (6/94, Concord CCD 4686) CD

Farr	Nick	Keep Moving (cdbaby.com)
Fasciani	Guy	Steinway Caper (TAPE)
Faye	Frances	No Reservations with Frances Faye(Capitol LP,T-512)
Feather	Leonard	(Decca 8088-Piano w. Dinah Washington in Lionel Hampton Concert)
Feinstein	Michael	Live at the Algonquin, Parnassus
Feldman	Victor	The Arrival Of V.F. (1/58, Original Jazz Classics OJC 268)
Felix	Lennie	L.F. at Nova Park, Zurich (1975, 88 Upright 003)
Fennell	David James	Over The Moon (cdbaby.com)
Ferrara	John	Intervals of Light (cdbaby.com)
Ferris	Christopher	A Chime In The Woods-2005 (cdbaby.com)
Fest	Manfredo	Jungle Cat (June 1989, DMP)
Few	Bobby	f -Steve Lacy: Live at Sweet Basil (Jul.6,7, 1991, Novus 3128; Novus 0647)
Fields	Harry	From Bach to Rock (10/63, Capitol Custom SUB-2237)
Fields	Andy	A.F.Somewhere in Time (cdbaby.com)
Fields	Irving	More Bagels and Bongos-Irving Fields Trio (Decca, DL-4114)
Finch	David	From The Heart (cdbaby.com)
Finn	Leo John	Cocktail Jazz (cdbaby.com)
Finn	Ellen Lippman	Matzoballs and Chitlins-A Tzimmes of Jewish /Jazz and Blues (cdbaby.com)

Finn	Mickey	M.F.with Cathy Reilly-Just Because (cdbaby.com)
Fiorenza	Lisa	Saturday Morning (cdbaby.com)
Fischer	Edna	Ragtime Piano Interpretations (Folkways RF 24)
Fischer	John	f- Duos for a New Decade (1977-8, Re-entry 004)
Fischer	Jim	New Road (cdbaby.com)
Fischer	Clare	Clare Fischer-The State of his Art (Revelation, R-26)
Fitch	Mal	Crewcuts (Emarcy 36041) singer, pianist, composer
Flahive	Larry	Century City Blues
Flanagan	Tommy	The T.F. Tokyo Recital (1975, Pablo 2310724)
Flannery	Molly	M.F.Quintet:Slow Dance at the Asylum (cdbaby.com)
Fleschner	Dave	At Home (cdbaby.com)
Flint	Ben	Onyx (cdbaby.com)
Florence	Bob	Sue Raney with B.F.-Flight of Fancy, Discovery
Florence	Henri	Chet Baker: All Blues (9/79, Arco 3 ARC 102)CD
Flores	George	Understanding Love (cdbaby.com)
Floyd	Bobby	Floyd's Finest Gift (cdbaby.com)
Flugge	Mark	February's Promise (cdbaby.com)
Fol	Raymond	Echoes of Harlem (1975, BStar 80702)

Folds	Chuck	CD's w. Rick Fay (Arbors), Cheatham (Columbia)
Foresythe	Reginald	Swing for Roundabout (1936, Decca F6203)Pianist, composer, bandleader
Forman	Mitch	Only A Memory (8/82, Soul Note SN 1070)
Forrester	Joel	CD's w. Micro.Spt. (Osmosis; Stash)
Foster	Herman	The Explosive Piano of H.F. (1961, Epic 17016)
Foster	Billy	B.F.Trio and Friends "Portrait" (cdbaby.com)
Fox	Donal	Gone City (5/94, New World NW 80515)CD
Fraga	Andy	Jazz in Palm Springs (cdbaby.com)
Franzetti	Carlos	Galaxy Dust (1979-80, IC 1113) Pianist & composer
Fraser	Hugh	Pas de Problemes (1989, CBC 2- 0119) CD- Pianist & Trombonist
FReDeRique		FReDeRique: Paris-New York…and Elsewhere (cdbaby.com)
Free	Stan	Piano a la Percussion-Stan Free (Old Town Records, LP-2002)
Freeman	Ernie	Ernie Freeman Plays-Dreaming With Freeman (Imperial, 12001)LP
Freeman	Stan	Piano Sweethearts (Columbia, Cl 1326)LP
Freeman	Russ	Shelly Manne & His Men Play More "Peter Gun" ('59, Contemporary, M-3566)
Freichel	Louis	Trummer Jazz: Jazz and Hot Dance After the Nazi's(1946-49,1987 Harl. 2052
Freitas	Richard	Tootsie Tunes (cdbaby.com)
French	Frank	James Scott's Ragtime (cdbaby.com)

Friedman	Don	D.F. Trio-Flashback, Riverside
Friedman	Janice	Finger Painting (1993, Jazzmania)
Frishberg	Dave	Live at Vine Street (Fantasy) vocalist & composer
Fritz	Ken	Dream Clouds (cdbaby.com)
Froeba	Frank (,Jr.)	In My Mizz (1938, Decca 1869) Pianist & bandleader
Frye	Don	Voulez-vous (1945, Disc 6009)
Fuhs	Julian	Ace in the Hole (1926, Elec. 386) Bandleader & pianist
Fujii	Satoko	Indication (May 17, 1996 & Sept.12, 1996, Libra)
Fulford	Tommy	Chick Webb: I ain't got nobody (1937, Decca 1513)
Funch		Sound Waves (1994, Funch JF2CF)
Funk	Joann	Solo Piano (cdbaby.com)
Futterman	Joel	Inner Conversations (10/84-6/88, Ear-Rational 1019)CD
Galian	Geri	Rhapsody in Rhythm (LXA 1001)
Galliher	Lucy	Live at Helen's (cdbaby.com)
Gallo	Ricardo	Loss Cerros Testigos (cdbaby.com)
Galper	Hal	H.G. at Maybeck-Volume 6, Concord,CCD4438
Gambrell	Freddie	F.G. with Ben Tucker, World Pacific
Ganelin	Vyacheslav	Von Anima (1977, Mel. C60073612) Pianist & composer

Gannon	Bill	Sweet Singing with the B.G. 3, Carlton
Gant	Cecil	Screwy Boogie (1944-50) Pianist & Singer
Garcia	Age	Alabastro (cdbaby.com)
Gardner	Jack	Doll Rag (1944, Steiner-Davis 508) Pianist & composer
Gardner	Jeff	Second Home (8/94, Musidisc 500722)CD
Gardner	Guy	Emma's Dream (cdbaby.com)
Gardony	Laszio	Changing Standards (Aug.15, 1990, Sunnyside)CD
Garfield	David	Giving Back (cdbaby.com)
Garisto	Lou	Metropolitan Jazz Quartet :Great Themes From Great Amer.Movie(MGM,E3727)
Garland	Red	Red in Blues-Ville, Prestige
Garner	Erroll	Concert by the Sea (Sept.19, 1955, Columbia)
Garr	Leonard	I Wish You Love (cdbaby.com)
Garrick	Michael	Mr.Smith's Apocalypse (1971, AGF1) Pianist, organist, composer
Garson	Mike	Avant Garson (Nov.20-21, 1979, Contemporary)
Gaslini	Giorgio	Gaslini Plays Monk (1981, SN 1020)
Gates	Russell	Music Alloy (cdbaby.com)
Gebert	Bobby	The Sculptor (1994, ABC Music)
Gee	Jonathan	Closer To (9/96, ASC CD14)CD

Geissendoerfer	Uli	The Extension (cdbaby.com)
Geller	Lorraine	Memorial (Freshsound) CD
Germanson	Rick	Rick Germanson Quintet-Heights (cdbaby.com)
Gershwin	George	G.G. Plays the Rhapsody in Blue, 20th Century Fox
Gerson	Roy	CD's w. Jazz Alliance (Led his own group-Swinglet)
Gessinger	Nils	Jam it Up! (cdbaby.com)
Gibson	Harry	Swingtime Jive, Stash
Gibson	Willie	Pseudonym for Lou Stein
Gibson	Professor Randy	Double Portion (cdbaby.com)
Gibson	Elmer	The E.G.Trio (cdbaby.com)
Gibson	Jim	Songs of the Civil War (cdbaby.com)
Gil	Robert	Art Pepper, Manne (Charlie Parker Records)
Gilman	Joe	Time Again:Brubeck Revisited (cdbaby.com)
Gilreath	Paul	The Eyes of the Morrow (cdbaby.com)
Gilson	Jef	Europamerica (1976, Palm 28)
Gioia	Ted	The End Of The Open Road (1988, Quartet)CD
Glanden	Don	Only Believe (1995,1997 Cadence JR 1093)CD(order thru Cadence)
Glantz	Lee	Love At First Glantz (cdbaby.com)

Glenn	Lloyd	Deep Blue Melody-with Don Albert (1936, Voc. 3423)
Glenn	Timothy	Composure (cdbaby.com)
Glik	Chris	Music for the Heart (cdbaby.com)
Gold	Sanford	Pianist d'or (c1955, Prst.7019)
Gold	Bob	Departures (cdbaby.com)
Gold	Loren	Keys (cdbaby.com)
Goldberg	Aaron	Empathy-Tony Gaboury (IM-2010) CD
Goldberg	Stu	Piru (1980, MPS 68262)
Goldings	Larry	Awareness (1997,Warners) also Organist
Goldkette	Jean	Bix Beiderbecke Vol. 2 (1927, Masters of Jazz)
Goldstein	Gil	City Of Dreams (3-7/89, Blue Note CDP 793893)CD
Goldstein	Jeff	The J.G.Group-Mount Jazz (cdbaby.com)
Gomez	Edsel	Cubist Music (cdbaby.com)
Gomez	Edsel Robert	CD's w. Byron (Nonesuch)
Gonzalez	Benitio	Starting Point (cdbaby.com)
Gordon	Bill	A Little Romance (cdbaby.com)
Gordon	Kimberly	Kim Gordon Trio-Melancholy Serenade (cdbaby.com)
Gore	Denny	Two For Dinner (cdbaby.com)

Gorrill	Liz	Dreamflight (5/90, New Artists NA 1010) CD- Pianist & Vocal
Goto	Sayuri	Flashback (cdbaby.com)
Gould	Tony	Best of Friends (1984, Move 3046)
Gould	Gretchen	Lonely Afternoon (cdbaby.com)
Graas	John	The J.G. Nonet- Jazzmantics, Decca
Grabowsky	Paul	Dale Barlow: Wizards of Oz (1988, Emarcy 834 531-2)
Graham	Oscar Bryant	Spirit of Love (cdbaby.com)
Graillier	Michael	Chet Baker: Mister B (Timeless SJP 192)CD
Grand	Mr.Baby	Soul of a Piano; Solo Piano (cdbaby.com)
Grant	Darrell Lemont	The New Bop (1996, Criss Cross)
Grant	Tom	Solo Piano (cdbaby.com)
Gratz	Reed	Below Sealevel (cdbaby.com)
Grauer	Joanne	Nine and a Half Weeks (Solo piano for film)
Graves	Conley	C.G. Trio- Piano Dynamics, Decca
Grawe	Georg	Flex 27 (12/93, Random Acoustics RA 007) CD
Gray	Reese	R.G. and The Sideways Alley Jazz Band:live at Henry's Bistro (cdbaby.com)
Gray	Owen	Mumbo Jumbo (cdbaby.com)
Green	Benny	Lineage (Jan.30, 1990-Feb.1,1990, Blue Note 93670)

Green	William	Magic Dream (cdbaby.com)
Green	Jesse	CD's w. Chiaro (1992)
Green	Johnny	Johnny Green On The Hollywood Stage (MGM, E-3694)
Greene	Bob	The World of Jelly Roll Morton (1974, RCA ARL1-0504)Pianist & bandleader
Greene	Burton	f- It's All One (1978, Horo 27-8)
Greensill	Michael	Lucky To Be Me (1989, Landmark, LLP 1524) accompanist for Weslia Whitfield
Greig	Stan	Blues Every Time (3/85, Calligraph CLG 004)
Greko	Keith	Buddy DeFranco/John Denman (Aug.1983, LUD 101)
Grolnick	Don	Nighttown (1992, BN)
Grossman	Richard	Trio in Real Time (10/89-1/90, Nine Winds NWCD 0134) CD
Group	White Tie	Plays Well With Others (cdbaby.com)
Grover	Steve	Steve Grover Trio-Breath (cdbaby.com)
Gruntz	George	Noon in Tunisia (1967, Saba 15132)
Grusin	Dave	Harlequin (c1984, GRP91015)Pianist, electronic keyboard,composer
Grusin	Don	Raven (1990, GRP)
Guaraldi	Vince	In Person (Dec.1962, Fantasy)
Guarnieri	Johnny	Gliss me Again, Classic Jazz
Guilaroff	Vera	Ragtime Piano Interpretations (Folkways RF 2)

Gulda	Friedrich	Fata Morgana-Friedrich Gulda live at the Domicile (April 1971, MPS, 68.060)
Gumbs	Onajee Allen	Onaje (1976, Ste. 1069)
Gumpert	Ulrich	Echos von Karolinenhof (1979, FMP0710)Pianist & composer
Guy	Aye	The Lester Young-Buddy Rich Trio (Norgran, MGN-1074)
Haddock	Russ	R.H. Trio- Appearing Nightly, Coral
Haig	Al	Piano Interpretation (June 21, 1976, Sea Breeze)
Hakim	Sadik	Memories (1978, Prog. 83)
Hale	Corky	Anita O'Day (Verve 2000)
Hale	Simon	East Fifteen (1992, EFZ)
Hall	Skip	Buddy Tate and his Celebrity Club Orch.(Vol. i,1954,BB33006)arrang, pno.,o.
Hall	Doug	Three Wishes (cdbaby.com)
Hall	Tammy	Blue Divine (cdbaby.com)
Hall II	Samuel Thomas	Play It Again Sam (cdbaby.com)
Hallas	Michael	The Lucidity Project (cdbaby.com)
Hallberg	Bengt	Hallberg's Surprise (3-5/87, Phontastic PHONT 7581)CD
Hamilton	Scrappy	Stay On Target (cdbaby.com)
Hammack	Karen	K.H./Paul Kriebibch Quartet: Lonesome Tree (cdbaby.com)
Hammer	Jan.	The First Seven Days (1975, Nemperor 432)

Hammer	Bob	CD's w. Mingus (Freshsound, Blue Note) composer & arranger
Hammer	Buck	The Discovery of Buck Hammer (Hanover-M 8001)(Steve Allen?)
Hammer	Tardo (Richard Alan)	CD's w. Doug Lawrence (Fable)
Hamp	Timothy	Hit The Keys (cdbaby.com)
Hampton	Kne-O'Chaw	From Deep In My Soul (cdbaby.com)
Hancock	Herbie	Maiden Voyage (1965, BN 84195)
Handy	George	Dalvajore Sally (1946, Jewell 1-1)arranger, composer, pianist
Hanna	Sir Roland	Perugia (1974, Freedom)
Hannemann	Daniel	Good News Piano (cdbaby.com)
Hansen	Ole Kock	Jazz Exchange (1975, Sto.1017)Pianist, arranger, composer
Hardcastle	Paul	The Very Best (1981-1989, EMI)
Harding	Buster (Lavere)	Compilations: The Indispensable Count Basie (1927-50)
Hargreaves	Sean	S.H.Trio-Rush Hour (cdbaby.com)
Haris	Niki	N.H. & Friends (cdbaby.com)
Harley	Cathy	Tuesday's Tune (2/95, Rufus RF 028)CD
Harley	Marvin	Just Me (cdbaby.com)
Harnell	Joe	I Want To Be Happy-Joe Harnell-Piano with Orchestra (Epic LP, BN-573)
Harris	Rick	Jazz Music Funk (cdbaby.com)

Harris	Ace	Lips Page- Rockin' at Ryan's (1944)
Harris	Arthur	Harris-Leigh: New Jazz in Hi-Fi (Epic LN 3200)
Harris	Barry	B.H. at Maybeck-Volume 12, Concord,CCD4476
Harris	Gene	Blue Genes-The Three Sounds (Oct.1962, Verve. V-8513)
Harrison	Michael Allen	Emotional Connection (cdbaby.com)
Harrison	Mark	M.H.Quintet-The Road Ahead (cdbaby.com)
Hart	Clyde	Ben Webster-The Horn (1944, Circle, CLP-41)
Hasan		Welcome To My World (cdbaby.com)
Hauck	Markus	Dancer in the Light (cdbaby.com)
Hawes	Hampton	Hampton Hawes Trio, Vol.1(June 28, 1955, Contemporary/OJC)
Hayes	Edgar	Blue Flame (1931, Bruns.6143)Pianist, arranger, bandleader
Haymes	Joe	He's the Life of the Party (1932, Vic.24052)Pianist & arranger
Haynes	Cyril	Slim Gailard-Laughing in Rhythm: Best of the Verve Yrs.('47-52, 314521651-2)
Hays	Kevin	Sweet Ear (1/91, Steeplechase SCCD 31282) CD
Hayton	Lennie	R.Nichols: Feelin' No Pain(1927, Bruns.3626)Pianist,composer,arranger
Hayward	Lance	Killing me Softly (1987, Island, 90683-1)
Haywood	Cedric	Kid Ory Plays W.C.Handy (1958, Verve 6061)
Hazeltine	David	D.H.Trio/Quartet- A World For Her (Criss 1170) CD

Hearn	Gloria	Master Jazz Piano Volume 3 (8/23/72, Swaggie S1337)
Henderson	Fletcher	Hocus Pocus (1934, Bb 5682) arranger
Henderson	Horace	H.H. 1940 (2-10/40, Tax M-8013)
Henderson	Lil	Jazz Women- A Feminist Retrospective, Stash
Henderson	Skitch	More Skitch Tonight (Columbia CS 9250)
Henderson	William H.	Solo Piano (cdbaby.com)
Henderson	Bobby	The Ruby Braff Octet w/P. Wee Russell & B.H.(1957,Verve Cleff, MGV8241)
Henke	Mel	M.H. Volume 2- Now Spin This!, Contemporary
Henne	Marty	The Songs You Know By The People You Don't (cdbaby.com)
Hennen	Mark	M.H./Toby Kasavian: Theory of Everything(duo pianists) (cdbaby.com)
Hennessey	Mike	The M.H. Chastet (10/3 & 4, 1993, In & Out Records IOR 7025-2)CD
Henning	Ann-Marie	Tidal Dreams (5-8/96, Dragon DRCD 279)CD
Henriksen	Bruno	Idano (1952, Phi.55002H) Pianist & bandleader
Hepler	David	Song For My Father (cdbaby.com)
Herbin	Frank	Ragtime Piano Novelties of the Twenties (Folkways RBF 42)
Herder	Paul	Meeting Life (cdbaby.com)
Hersch	Fred	Forward Motion (1991, Chesky 55)
Herskowitz	Matt	Forget Me Not (cdbaby.com)

Herzig	Monika	M.H. Acoustic Project: Melody With Harmony (cdbaby.com)
Hess	Cliff	Ragtime Piano Interpretations (Folkways RF 24)
Hewitt	Lonnie	Live and Direct-Cal Tjader Quintet (Fantasy, F 8059)LP
Hewitt	Frank	We Loved You (cdbaby.com)
Heywood	Eddie	The Touch of E.H.. RCA
Hicks	John	J.H. at Maybeck-Volume 7, Concord,CCD4442
Higbie	Barbara	I Surrender (cdbaby.com)
Higgins	Eddie	Soulero (August 25, 1965, Atlantic)
Higgins	Sean	The New Thought (cdbaby.com)
Hill	Alex	Duos with J.Wells:Stompin' em Down/Tack Head Blues(1929,Voc1270)
Hill	Andrew	Invitation-Andrew Hill Trio (Oct.1974, Inner City, 2026)
Hillman	Charles	Ole Miss Rag(9/22/17-77362-3- Columbia A2420)Side 53B-Franklin Mint Jazz
Hilton	Lisa	In The Mood For Jazz (cdbaby.com)
Hines	Earl "Fatha"	Live at Buffalo (1976, Improv)
Hinkley	Tim	Janie Akin: Travelin' Woman (cdbaby.com)
Hipp	Jutta	J.H. at the Hickory House (1956, BN 1515-16)
Hitchings	David	Passion Voyage (cdbaby.com)
Hobizal	Edward	Anamnesis (cdbaby.com)

Hodes	Art	A.H.:South Side Memories (1983, Sack. 3032)
Hoff	Jan Gunnar	Moving (4/94-2/95, Curling Legs CLP CD16)CD
Hoffer	Frederick	CD5,Piano Suite Number Four (cdbaby.com)
Hoffman	Ingfried	From Ywen with Love (1966, Phi.843779)Pianist & organist
Hoffman	Ellen	Daydreams (cdbaby.com)
Hoffman	Marc	Long Way Home (cdbaby.com)
Holmes	Richard "Groove"	Hot Tat (9/89, Muse M 5395)CD; organist
Holmes	Joel	Eternal Vision (cdbaby.com)
Holober	Michael	CD's w. Brignola (Reservoir)
Holt	Stanley C.	Ragtime Piano Novelties of the Twenties (Folkways RBF 42)
Holt	Steve	S.H./Kieran Overs: Just Duet (cdbaby.com)
Holzman	Adam	Overdrive (1991-92, Lipstick LIP 890252) CD
Honda	Takehiro (Takashi)	CD's w. JVC; Funhouse
Hoopes	Ronnie	Respect for a Great Tradition, Revelation
Hope	Bertha	Between Two Kings (1992, Minor Music 801025) CD
Hope	Elmo	Last Sessions- Vol. 2, Inner City
Hopkins	Claude	Crazy Fingers (1972, Chiaroscuro, Chi.114)
Hopkins	Colin	Peter Knight Quartet-between two moments (cdbaby.com)

Horiuchi	Glenn	Poston Sonata (Dec.1991, Asianimprov)
Horler	John	Lost Keys (5/93, Master Mix CHECD00109) CD
Horn	Shirley	Close Enough For Love (Nov. 1998, Verve)
Horowitz	David	Svengali (1973, Atl.1643)
Horrox	Frank	Lullaby of Birdland (1953, Decca F10200)
Horvitz	Wayne	Miracle Mile (1991, Electra Nonesuch 7559)CD
Hostage	Peter	P.H.Trio-Do That! (cdbaby.com)
Houston	John	Curtis Amy: Tippin' on Through (1962, PJ 62)
Howard	Bob	Swing it Bob (1936, Bruns.02230, 02239)Singer & pianist
Howard	Camille	Rock Me Daddy (1947-52, Specialty 7046)
Howrani	Waleed	Firedance (cdbaby.com)
Hug	Armand	A.H. Plays Armand Piron (1953, Para. 114)
Hughes	Fred	Ricky Loza-My Dreams (Jazz Karma JKR915) CD
Hulse	Steve	Jazzed For The Beatles (cdbaby.com)
Hundley	Craig	C.H. Trio- Arrival of a Young Giant, World Pacific
Hunt	Brendon	Renew (cdbaby.com)
Hunt	Fred	Pearls on Velvet (1968, 77 LEU27)
Hunt	Steve	From Your Heart and Your Soul (cdbaby.com)

Hunter	T.Storm	Harem-Scarem Suite (cdbaby.com)
Huntley	Robert	Here Now (cdbaby.com)
Hutchinson	Andrew	A.H.Trio-Lost But Not Forgotten (cdbaby.com)
Hutslar	Calet	Calet Hutslar (cdbaby.com)
Hyman	Dick	Genius at Play, Monmouth Evergreen
Iago	Weber	Spring Will Stay Here (cdbaby.com)
Ibrahim	Abdullah	This is Dollar Brand (Mar.1965, Black Lion, BL-192)
Ignatzek	Klaus	Magic Secret (1/85, Nabel 4617)CD
Ikawa	Yayoi	Color of Dreams (cdbaby.com)
Illwill		Round 2 (cdbaby.com)
Ingham	Keith	(EMI) Solo
Intini	Cosmo	Seeing The Cosmic (11/86, Splasc(h) H 121)
Intra	Enrico	CD's -Dire; Ed. Paoline; w. Jazz Class Orch., Intra & L. Konitz, Guests
Iversen	Elnar	Me and My Piano (1967, Nor-Disc. LPS 17)Pianist & flutist
Iverson	Ethan	Deconstruction Zone (Standards)-(4/98, Fresh Sound FSNT 047)CD
Jackson	Calvin	Rave Notice, Columbia
Jackson	Cliff	Carolina Shout (1962 & 1964, Black Lion)
Jackson	D.D.	Peace-Song (11/94, Justin Time JUST 72) CD

Jackson	Tyrone	Dedicated (cdbaby.com)
Jacob	Christian	Time Lines (cdbaby.com)
Jacobs	Pim	Come Fly With Me (1982, Phi. 6423529)
Jacobs	Cori	Copperskin (cdbaby.com)
Jacobson	Pete	Bobby Wellin Quartet: Jubilation (1978, Vortex 1)
Jaffe	Nat	How Can You Face Me? /Keepin' out of Mischief Now(1944, Sig.28112)
Jagodzinski	Andrzej	Chopin (12/93, Polonia CD 022) CD
Jamal	Ahmad	Ahmad Jamal At The Pershing:But Not For Me (Jan.16, 1958, Cadet)
James	Bob	Hands Down (1982, Tappan Zee, FC38067)
James	Richard	As In A Dream (cdbaby.com)
Jang	Jon	Self Defense! (6/91, Soul Note 121203) CD
Jankowski	Horst	Jankows Keyboard (1971, MPS 3320880)Pianist & bandleader
Jansen	Nadine	A Little Taste (1990, Jantone)
Janssen	Guus	On the Line (1979, Claxon 4)
Jansson	Lars	A Window Towards Being (2/91, Imogena IGCD 019)CD
Janzen	Mike	M.J.Trio-Beginnings (cdbaby.com)
Ja-Paul		Ja-Paul-Count Down (cdbaby.com)
Jarrett	Keith	Invocations(1979-80, ECM 1201-2)

Jarvis	Jayne	The Jane Jarvis L.A. Quartet (2/88, Audiophile ACD 248)CD
Jarvis	Jon	The John Jarvis Trio-Hear No Evil (Oct.21-23, 1998, TVT Jazz)CD
Jasperse	Greg	Tournesol (cdbaby.com)
Javors	Keith	Mo' City Jungle (cdbaby.com)
Jaxen	Kazzrie	Prayers & Mad Laughter (cdbaby.com)
Jazz	Sweet	Sweet Jazz: Romantic Impressions (cdbaby.com)
Jazzphilosophy		Jazz Trio (cdbaby.com)
Jean-Marie	Alain	Latin Alley (1987, IDA 015)CD
Jenkins	Arty	Sabu's Jazz Espagnole (EAB-145)
Jenkins	Billy	v- Piano Sketches : 1973-84 (73-84, Wood Wharf WWR 841)
Jentes	Harry	Ragtime Piano Novelties of the Twenties (Folkways RBF 42)
Jeon	Hey Rim	H.R.J. & Friends (cdbaby.com)
Jetro	Duke	Worry, Worry, Worry (11/21/64-ABC Paramount 509) 56B-Franklin Mint Jazz
Jezek	Jaroslav	Echoes of Prague Music Hall ('30-38, Sup.10132887)Pno., composer,arranger
Jivestone		Jivestone (cdbaby.com)
Jobim	Antonio Carlos	Wave (May 22-24, 1967, A & M)
Jocko	Jackie	Jackie Jocko, Piano And Vocals (Strand, SLS1053)LP
Joel	Billy	B.J.-Piano Man, Columbia

Johansson	Ake	Encore (8/87, Dragon DRLP 159)
Johansson	Jens	Ten Seasons (cdbaby.com)
Johansson	Jan	Live in Tallinn (cdbaby.com)
John	Dr.	In a Sentimental Mood (1989, WB 9 25889-2)
Johnson	Tommy	Bare Naked Boogie (cdbaby.com)
Johnson	Buddy	Shufflin' And Rollin' (1952, Decca 28293) Bandleader
Johnson	Charlie	Harlem Drag (1929, Victor 38059)Pianist & bandleader
Johnson	Dink	B. Campbell & D.J.:The Professors('64, Euphonic 1201-2)Pno.,clarinetist,drums
Johnson	Freddy	Harlem Bound (1933, Bruns. A500340) Band Pianist
Johnson	James P.	Here is J.P.J. at his rare of all rarest performances-Vol.1, Kings of Jazz
Johnson	Margaret	Billy Holiday's Orch. with Lester Young in N.Y. (Sept.1938- 4 titles)
Johnson	Pete	Pete's Blues/Let 'em Jump (1939, Solo Art 12005)
Johnson	Sy	w. Charles Mingus-Let My Children Hear Music (1971)
Johnson	Hank	The H.J. Trio (cdbaby.com)
Johnson	Eustace	Hyms I Love To Play-Vol.1 (cdbaby.com)
Johnson	Greg	G.J. and Glass Brick Boulevard-Life As Essential Experience (cdbaby.com)
Johnson	Daryl	From the Middle (cdbaby.com)
Johnson	Deron	Silent Knight (cdbaby.com)

Johnson	Kevin	Symbolism & Ceremony (cdbaby.com)
Jolly	Pete	Herb Alpert Presents Pete Jolly (1968, A & M)
Jolly	Bill	Behind the Scarf (cdbaby.com)
Jones	Jazzou	The Riverboat Ragtime- Then & Now (cdbaby.com)
Jones	Curtis	Bedside Blues (1941) Pianist & Blues Singer
Jones	Dill	The Music of Bix Beiderbecke (1972, Chi. 112)
Jones	Hank	Just For Fun (June 27-28, 1977, Galaxy)
Jones	Jimmy	J.J.Trio (1954, Swing 33336)
Jones	Michael	Live at Steinway Hall(1999, Chiaroscuro:ASIN: BOOYHYGC)
Jones	Oliver	Speak Low-Swing Hard (1986, Justin Time)
Jones	Richard M.	Jazzin' Babies Blues/ Twelfth Street Rag (1923, Gen.5174)
Jones III	Warren	Bridges (cdbaby.com)
Joplin	Scott	Elite Syncopations: Classic Ragtime from Rare Piano Rolls(Bio.110)
Jordan	Kim	Full Circle (cdbaby.com)
Jordan	Duke	les liasons dangereuses-Duke Jordan (1962, Charlie Parker, PLP-813)
Jorgensen	Knud	Knud Jorgensen Jazz Trio (Opus 3, 8401)LP
Joseph	Julian	The Language Of Truth (1991, East West 75122-2)CD
Joseph	Paul	P.J.Trio- Yes and No (cdbaby.com)

Joslin	Perry	P.J.Project (cdbaby.com)
Josquin	Christoph	Early in the Morning (cdbaby.com)
K	Randell	Randell K (cdbaby.com)
Kahn	George	Midnight Brew (cdbaby.com)
Kahsen	Jhon	Love's Bitter Rage (cdbaby.com)
Kamenir	David	There Are No Delis In Ensenada (cdbaby.com)
Kano	Misako	3 Purple Circles (JFCD03Y) Jazz Focus CD
Kantonen	Seppo	Klang (Impala 001)CD
Kaper	Bronislaw	The Film Music of B.K. played by the composer, Delos
Kapstad	Egil	Cherokee (11/88, Gemini GMED 61) CD
Karashima	Fumio	Transparent (1987, Pol. H33P20149)
Karayorgis	Pandelis	In Time (April 1993, Leo)
Karlson	Jacob	Take Your Time! (5/95, Dragon DRCD 276)CD
Karlsson(Nils)	Stefan	Room 292; CD's: Just; w. Sebastian Whittaker (Just.)
Karolak	Wojciech	The Karolak Trio (1962, Muza 0200)
Karush	Larry	The Art of The Improvisor (5/97, Naxos 86026 2)CD
Kaspersen	Jan.	Live In Sofie's Cellar (8/91, Olufsen DOCD 5136)CD
Kassoff	Russ	Bucky Pizzarelli: The Cafe Pierre Trio(Aug.25 & 26, 1982,ME7093)

Kater	Peter	Piano (cdbaby.com)
Katindig	Boy	Groovin' High (cdbaby.com)
Katsenelenbogen	Eyran	Solotude (cdbaby.com)
Katz	Bruce	Transformation (11/93, Audioquest AQ CD1026) CD
Katz	Jonathan	Continuance (cdbaby.com)
Katz	Dick	Piano & Pen-Dick Katz (Atlantic, 1314)
Kawaguchi	Yoko	Before It's Too Late (cdbaby.com)
Kawahara	Shigeki	Another World (cdbaby.com)
Kaye	Joshua	The J.K. Quartet Live (cdbaby.com)
Keenan	Brian	Hidden Falls (cdbaby.com)
Keezer	Geoff	Here and Now (Oct.1990, Blue Note 96691)
Kellaway	Roger	Ain't Misbehaven (Feb.1986, Choice)
Keller	Sue	Ol' Muddy (1993, Ragtime Press)
Keller	Sue	a.k.a.Charles Johnson(ragtime piano)-"A Little Lost Lamb" (cdbaby.com)
Kelley	Peck	P.K. Jam (1983, Com. 625527-8)
Kelly	Daniel	World (cdbaby.com)
Kelly	Ed	Ed Kelly and Pharoah Sanders (12/78-12/92, Evidence ECD22056-2)CD
Kelly	Mark	Broken Fingers (cdbaby.com)

Kelly	Brian	Pools of Light (cdbaby.com)
Kelly	Wynton	New Faces-New Sounds-Wynton Kelly (Blue Note 10", BLP-5025)
Kemp	Emme	Try a LIttle Tenderness (cdbaby.com)
Kendrick	Rodney	Dance World Dance (12/93, Verve 521937) CD
Kennedy	Ray	CD's w. Pizzarelli (RCA)
Kenton	Stan	Kenton's West Side Story(Capitol, T-1609)
Kerr	Brooks Jr.	Soda Fountain Rag (1975, Chi. 2001); LP's own Blue Wail Label
Kersey	Ken	It Might As Well Be Spring-Sol Yaged his clarinet & quintet (Herald, HLP-0103)
Khan	Steve	Evidence (1980, AN3023)
Khoeblal	Sonny	Wings of Peace (cdbaby.com)
Khu	Art	Reconciliation (cdbaby.com)
Kikoski	David	Presage (7-8/84, Freelance FRL 011)CD
Kikuchi	Masabumi	One Way Traveler (1980, CBS 25AH1402)
Kimbrough	Frank Marshall Jr.	Marian McPartland's Piano Jazz '97; CD's w. Rich Perry (Steep.)
King	John	In From the Cold (1/94, Criss Cross- CRISS 1093) CD
Kirkland	Kenny	Kenny Kirkland (1991, GRP)
Kirkpatrick	Don	The Fabulous Sidney Bechet and his Hot Six with Sidney DeParis(BN7020)
Kishino	Yoshiko	Photograph (3/96, GRP 98842)CD

COMPENDIUM OF OVER 2000 JAZZ PIANISTS

Klein	Phil	Unforgettable Love Songs (cdbaby.com)
Knudsen	Kenneth	Bombay Hotel (10/88, Stunt Records 18903)CD
Knutson	Mary Louise	Call Me When You Get There (cdbaby.com)
Kobayashi	Ron	R.K.Trio-Exotic Places (cdbaby.com)
Kocour	Mike	The M.K. Trio- High Standards (cdbaby.com)
Koenigsberg	Toby	T.K.Trio Special Guest Rich Perry-Push (cdbaby.com)
Kokubu	Hiroko	More Than You Know (1988, JVC)CD
Komeda	Krzysztof	Astigmatic (12/65, PowerBros 00125) CD
Korman	Cliff	Paraiso-Jazz Brazil (1993, Telarc-G.Mulligan with J.Duboc,CD83361)
Korossy	Janos	Korossy Janos es Egyuttes (1964, Qual. LPX 7301)
Kral	Roy	Jackie & Roy-Concerts By The Sea (Sept.1976, Studio 7, ST 7-402)
Krall	Diana	Stepping Out (1993, Just in Time)
Kramer	Mark	The M.K. Trio Album, Audophile
Kucij	Tim	Lifesongs (cdbaby.com)
Kuhn	Joachim	f- Piano (1971, MPS 2121330-7)
Kuhn	Steve	S.K. at Maybeck-Volume 13, Concord,CCD4484
Kulpowicz	Slawomir	Loaded (1979, Leo 010)
Kuniyoshi	Akemi	ARP Music (Leo Lab CD 004) CD

Kurlewicz	Andrzej	10 + 8 (1967, Muza 0439)
Kuryokhin	Sergey	Some Combinations of Fingers & Passion(1991, EEO LRCD178)CD-solo
Kyle	Billy	Sundays are reserved/Havin' a Ball (1937, Var. 574)
Kynard	Charles	o-Reelin' With the Feelin'/Wa-Ta-Zui(8/69-71, BGP CDBGPD 055CD)CD
Lackner	Benny	B.L.Trio-Sign of the Times (cdbaby.com)
LaCroix	Lise	L.L. & Friends (cdbaby.com)
Lacy	Butch	Chet Baker: When Sunny Gets Blue (2/86, Steeplechase 1221)CD
Ladd	Ray	A Nice Ladd, Miracle
LaForge	Jack	Promise Her Anything, Regina
Lahm	David	CD's : Ark.; Generation
Lahue	Michael A.	Sonho (cdbaby.com)
Lalama	Dave	CD's w. W. Herman (ITM; Conc.)
Lamaestra	Dan	D.L. and One Step Up- Just A Thought (cdbaby.com)
Lambert	Donald	Meet the Lamb (1961-62, ARC) CD
Lamka	Nancy	Heartcry (cdbaby.com)
Lande	Art	Hardball! (GAMH)
Landl	Ernst	Rug Cutters Swing (1944, ES 8120)
Landon	Louis	Love Songs & Jazz (cdbaby.com)

Lane	Barbara	Someone (cdbaby.com)
Lane	Beth	Lies of Handsome Men (cdbaby.com)
Lang	Mike	Electric Bath-The Don Ellis Orchestra (Columbia LP,CS-9585)
Lange	Henry	Ragtime Piano Interpretations (Folkways RF 24)
Lanoue	Conrad	Boogie Woogie (1939, Bb 10296) Pianist & arranger
Lantner	Steven	Reaching (8/97, Leo Lab 062)CD
Larkins	Ellis	Ellis Larkins: A Smooth Tone (July 1977, Classic Jazz, CJ-145)
Larsson	Rolf	Swing and Dance (1972, Polar 248)
Larue	Lisa	That ol' Sofkee Spoon (cdbaby.com)
Lausen	Jorgen	Jorgen Ryg Jazz Quartet (Mercury, MG-36099)
LaVere	Charlie	Chicago in the 30s (1935, Tax M8007)Pianist, bandleader, singer
LaVerne	Andy	A.L. at Maybeck-Volume 28, Concord,CCD4577
Law	John	Exploded on Impact (2 & 7/92, Slam CD 204) CD
Lawnhurst	Vee	Ragtime Piano Interpretations (Folkways RF 24)
Lawrence	Elliot	Elevation (1949, Col.38497) Bandleader, arranger, composer, pianist
Lawson	Hugh	Prime Time(1977,Sto.4708)
Lawton	Tom	Al Stauffer Trio-Things Ain't What They Used To Be(93,Plattonic PR1193-1)
Leake	Brian	Benign Jazz (1993, Inxent)

Leake	Max	Trios (cdbaby.com)
Leavell	Chuck	Forever Blue (cdbaby.com)
Ledgerwood	Lee Ann	You Wish (1991, Triloka)
Ledonne	Mike	Soulmates (1/93, Criss Cross 1074)CD
Ledwith	Ed	Find Me (cdbaby.com)
Lee	Dave	New Big Band From Britain (1960's) Pno., Arranger, Composer, Vocals, Leader
Lee	Julia	Draggin' My Heart Around (1949, Cap. 70051) Pianist & singer
Lee	Tony	Street of Dreams (1979, Lee Lambert 102)
Lee	Gordon	One Two Three (cdbaby.com)
Lee	Stephanie	One Little Seed (cdbaby.com)
Legge	Wade	C.Mingus: The Clown (1957, Atl. 1260)
Legrand	Michel	Legrand Piano-Michel Legrand and his Trio (Columbia, CL-1441)
Leighton	Rupert	Beyond Reflection (cdbaby.com)
Leighton	Bernie	The B.L. Quartet plays Duke Ellington (Monmouth-Evergreen,MES-7068)
Leijah		Perfect Love (cdbaby.com)
Lemer	Pete	Local Colour (1966, ESP 1057)
Lemieux	Mike	As You Wish (cdbaby.com)
Lemmon	Jack	Jack Lemmon sings and plays music from "Some Like It Hot" (Epic, LN-3559)

Lemon	Brian	Our Kind of Music (1970, 77 LEV38)
Leogrande	Dennis	Yesterday Once More (cdbaby.com)
Leon	Freddie	Moments (cdbaby.com)
Leonard	Alex	Down In The Depths: Interpretation of Cole Porter (cdbaby.com)
Leonhardt	David Emil	CD's w. M. Hendricks (Muse)
Lerner	Al	Ivory & Bone-Al Lerner (Roulette, R25124)LP
Lerner	Marilyn	Birds Are Returning (1/97, Jazz Focus JFCD 022)CD
LeSage	Bill	Martin Drew & His Band (1977, Lee Lambert 003)Pianist & vibraphonist
Lester	Billy	Captivatin' Rhythm (1985-95, Zinnia 108) CD
LeVan	Michael	Hands On (cdbaby.com)
Leviev	Milcho	Jazz Focus (1968, Saba 15219)
Levin	Adam	Things Left Unsaid (cdbaby.com)
Levine	Mark	Up' Til Now (1976, Cat. 7614) Pianist & trombonist
Levine	Douglas	Kromatica (cdbaby.com)
Levinovsky	Nikolay	Sfinks (Sphinx; 1986, Mel. C6024695003) Pianist & composer
Levy	Lou	Lou Levy-Touch of Class (Dobre, DR-1042)
LeWinter	David	Piano Pastels, EP-Mercury
Lewis	Meade Lux	The Blues Piano Artistry of Meade Lux Lewis (Nov.1, 1961, Riverside/OJC)

Lewis	Sabby	Edna (1946, Contl 6035) Pianist, bandleader, arranger
Lewis	Judy	Prayer in Black & White (cdbaby.com)
Lewis	John	MJQ Live At The Lighthouse (1967, Atlantic, SD-1486)
Lewis	Ramsey	The Movie Album Starring Ramsey Lewis (Cadet, LPS-782)
Libano	Guilo	Chet Baker With Fifty Italian Strings(9/59, OJC 492)CD
Lightsey	Kirk	Chet Baker: Everything Happens to Me(3/83, Timeless SJP 176)CD
Lindberg	Nils	Alone With My Melodies (4/95, Dragon DRCD 277) CD
Lindemann	Francois	Different Masks (10/89, Planisphare 1267-47)CD
Lindner	Craig	Blue Serenity (cdbaby.com)
Lindquist	Robert	2 Days and a Night (cdbaby.com)
Lingle	Paul	Dance of the Witch Hazels (1951, Euphonic)
Linkola	Jukka	Pegasos (11/93, Imogena IGCD 050) CD
Linton	Staffan	Unfinished Affair (3/90, Dragon DRCD 193)CD
Lipscomb	Dan	Sister Kate (April 1928-20470-7, Paramount 12640) 65A-Franklin Mint Jazz
Lipskin	Mike	M.L. with Willie "The Lion" Smith:California Here I Come(Fly.Dutchman)
Little	Dudley	Big Tiny Little-Movin' On (Coral, CRL 57425)LP
Litton	Martin	M.L. Jazz (1992, Solo Art)
Livingston	Marsha	At Last (cdbaby.com)

Lloyd	Paticia	P.L.Sings Music From Heaven (cdbaby.com)
Locascio	Joe	Home (cdbaby.com)
Lofton	Cripple Clarence	I Don't Know, Policy Blues (1943)
Londy		In My Life (cdbaby.com)
Longhair	Professor	AKA-Henry Roeland Byrd-The Big Easy ('49,1977,Blue Moon 094) Pno., & Vocal
Longo	Michael	The Awakening (Oct. 1972, Mainstream)
Lopez	Rodrigo	Life Experience (cdbaby.com)
Lopez Furst	Ruben	Jazz Argentino (1966, CBS 8695) Pianist & guitarist
Lorber	Jeff	The J.L. Fusion (1977, IC 1026)
Lord	Vivian	Two For The Road(1993, Stash)
Losito	Dino	Like That (cdbaby.com)
Louiss	Eddy	Our Kind of Sabi (1958, Verve 2304041)Pianist, organist,leader
Loussier	Jacques	Jacques Loussier Trio/Play Bach/5 (London, PS-524)
Lovett	Leroy	Ben Webster-Harry Carney with Strings(Verve reissued 314527774-2)
Lovitt	Michael	The Ship Of Fools (cdbaby.com)
Luck	Richard	Shanghai (cdbaby.com)
Ludvik	Emil	Inspiration (1940, Cesky Jazz 1913-1959,Sup. DV101778H)Pno.,arranger
Luevano	Dan	Simpler Time (cdbaby.com)

Lugo	Jose	Piano con mata (cdbaby.com)
Luijt	Eric Van	Express Yourself (cdbaby.com)
Lundgren	Jan.	Conclusion (5-6/94, Four Leaf Clover FLC CD 136) CD
Lutcher	Nellie	Women in Jazz- Pianists, Stash
Lyall	Chick	Solitary Dance (1/98, Caber 004)CD
Lyle	Bobby	Ivory Dreams, Atlantic
Lyon	Jimmy	J.L. Plays Cole Porter's Steinway and his Music (1982, Finnadar, SR-9034)
Mabern	Harold	Joy Spring (1/85, Sackville 2016)
Macdonald	Glyn	G.M.Trio (cdbaby.com)
MacDonald	Keith	This is Keith MacDonald (1984, Landmark, LLP-503)
MacDonough	Bill	B.D.Quartet- House of Jade (cdbaby.com)
Maceo	Big	Chicago Breakdown (RCA Victor)
MacKay	Dave	D.M. & Lori Bell Sextet-Take Me to Brazil (May 4-5,1988, Discovery)CD
Mackenzie	David	D.M. & Josh Johnston- A Minor Happiness (cdbaby.com)
Maclean	Leslie	L.M.Trio: That's Time Enough (cdbaby.com)
MacRae	Dave	Mike Westbrook: Love/Dream and Variations (Citadel/Room 315)
Madna	Rob	The Cool Voice of Rita Reys (Columbia, CL 903)LP
Madoca		Mysterious Ways (cdbaby.com)

Madsen	Peter	Snuggling Snakes (12/92, Minor Music 801030) CD
Magnes	Liz	L.M. & Sandra Bendor-Two White Mothers(duo pianists) (cdbaby.com)
Maguire	Alex	Live at Oscar's- A.M. & Steve Noble (1987, Incus) Pianist, Composer
Mahones	Gildo	The Soulful Piano of G.M. (1963-4, Prst. T339)
Mahrer	Randy	Pieces for the Portrat (cdbaby.com)
Makowicz	Adam	From My Window, Choice
Malachi	John	S.Vaughan: Swingin' Easy (1954, Ema 36109)
Malcolm	Horace	Jazz Gillium-You Are Doing Me Wrong (1937-41) Accompanied Blues Singers
Malinverni	Pete	CD's: SB; Res.
Malone	Bob	Born Too Late (cdbaby.com)
Malone	James	Shoot For The Moon (cdbaby.com)
Managan	Bill	Unlikely Pianist Unwinds (cdbaby.com)
Mance	Junior	The Soul of Hollywood, Jazzland
Mancini	Henry	Combo! Henry Mancini and His Orchestra (1961, RCA, LPM-2258)
Mandell	Ric	A Road Less Traveled (cdbaby.com)
Mandt	Chuck	Contemporary Sounds of Gospel Favorites (cdbaby.com)
Manetta	Manuel 'Fess'	Original Tuxedo Rag (1925, OK 8215)Pianist, cornetist, saxophonist
Mangione	Gap	Hey Baby! (1961, Riv. 9371)

Mann	Martan	Clazzical Jazz (cdbaby.com)
Manson	Bevan	Jazz A La Carte (cdbaby.com)
Mantooth	Frank	Dangerous Precedent (12/91, Sea Breeze SB 2046) CD
Manusardi	Guido	So That (10/90, Splasc(h) H-328)CD
Marable	Fate	Rec. Two Titles with his band: "Frankie and Johnny" & "PianoFlage"(1924, OK)
Marbach	Bob	Out at Night (cdbaby.com)
Marcotulli	Rita	Night Caller (1992, Label Bleu LBLC 6551) CD
Maria	Tania	Piquant (Dec.1980, Concord Jazz)
Marineau	Mark	Sound and Resonance (cdbaby.com)
Marion	Bruce	Sunsets: The Piano Collection (cdbaby.com)
Markaverich	Mike	Solid (cdbaby.com)
Markovitz	Phil	Chet Baker in Paris Volume 2(6/78, West Wind 2059)CD
Marks	Lydia	Lovelight Shinning (cdbaby.com)
Marlowe	Christopher	Nancy LaMott-Beautiful Baby (1991, Midder)CD
Marmarosa	Dodo	Dodo's Back! (1961, Argo 4012)
Marsalis	Ellis	Heart of Gold (1991, Columbia 47509)CD
Martin	Peter	CD's w. 4-Sight (N2K)
Martin	Christopher	New Vintage (cdbaby.com)

Martin	Ralph	Skin Deep-Louis Bellson and his orchestra (Norgran, MG N-1046)
Martinez	Conrad	Rex Stewart 1948-1949 (Classics 1164)CD
Marx	Dick	Too Much Piano-Dick Marx and John Frigo (Brunswick, BL-54006)
Mas	Jean-Pierre	Rue de Lourmel (2/76, Inner City IC 1014)
Maslov	Eugene	Where the Light Comes From (cdbaby.com)
Masman	Theo Uden	Ramblers Alabama Swing (1933-35, Panachord 2004)Bandleader & pianist
Masuda	Mikio	Trace (1974, EW 7004)
Mathews	Ronnie	Dark Before The Dawn (10/90, DIW 604)CD
Mathisen	Leo	A Wee Bit of Swing (1941, Odeon D515)Pno., singer ,bandleader,composer
Matni	Safwan	Dunya (cdbaby.com)
Matthews	Onzy Durrett Jr.	CD's w. Lou Rawls (Cap.); Pianist, vocal, arranger
Mattos	Angel David	Danzzaj (cdbaby.com)
Mauro, Jr.	Haroldo	Bossa na Pressao (cdbaby.com)
Maxted	Billy	Crosby's Great Hits (1960. Dot 25278)Pianist & arranger
Maycock	George	Maycock's Bop (1956, Phi. 47001)
Mayer	Jon	Rounding Up The Usual Suspects (1994, Pullen Music)
Mayerl	Billy	Ragtime Piano Novelties of the Twenties (Folkways RBF 42)
Mayers	Lloyd	A Taste of Honey (1962, UA 15018)

Mays	Lyle	As Falls Wichita, so Falls Wichita Falls(1980, 1190),ECM
Mays	Bill	Crystal Comments-Bud Shank-B.M.-Alan Broadbent (1979, Concord, CJ-126)
Mazzarino	Giovanni	Silence Please! (1/91, Splasc(h) H 375-2) CD
Mcauliffe	Heather	Heart's Desire (cdbaby.com)
McCann	Les	Les McCann The Man (1978, A & M, SP-4718)
McClerkin	Corky	Island of Dreams (cdbaby.com)
McCoy	Patti Moran	The Gospel Truth (cdbaby.com)
McDaniel	Willard	T.Bone Shuffle (Nov.1947-BW 662-Commett-53)Side 56B-Franklin Mint Jazz
McDonald	Tim	Tim McDonald (cdbaby.com)
McDonas	Thollem	Solo Piano (cdbaby.com)
McDonough	Larry	Small Steps (cdbaby.com)
McDuff	Jack	o-Prelude (1963, Prst. 7333)
McGrath	Fulton	Mystery/Tap Room Blues (1935, Decca 625)
Mcgregor	Chris	Blue Notes in Concert (1978, OGUN800)
McGriff	Jimmy	o-Blues for Mr. Jimmy, 1965, Sue 1039)
McGuffie	Bill	On Stage/Benny Goodman/Sextet: (Oct.1972, London BP44182/83)
McHugh	Bob	American Classics (cdbaby.com)
McKenna	Dave	By Myself-Dave McKenna (1976, Shiah, McKenna-1)

McKenzie	Al	Is It Love (cdbaby.com)
McKinney	Carlos	CD's: Sirocco Jazz; w. Buster Williams (Jazzline)
McLeish	Bertram	Say Beautiful Things (cdbaby.com)
McManus	Jill	Symbols of Hopi (1984); LP's: Conc., Muse
McNeely	Jim	J.M. at Maybeck-Volume 20, Concord,CCD4522
McPartland	Marian	The Marian McPartland Trio (July 1956, Capitol, T-785)
McPherson	Rod	100 Years Old (cdbaby.com)
McQuade	Scott	Life Just Couldn't Be Better (cdbaby.com)
McRae	George	Solitary Persuassions (cdbaby.com)
McShann	Jay	Swingmatism/Vine Street Boogie(1941, Decca 8570)
Meade	Glenn	Open Road-Suite for Jazz Piano (cdbaby.com)
Mechem	Lori	Shiny Stockings-The L.M.Quartet Plays Count Basie (cdbaby.com)
Medland	Logan	Something in Blue (cdbaby.com)
Mehegan	John	How I Play Jazz Piano-John Mehegan (1957, Savoy, MG-12076)
Mehldau	Brad	Introducing Brad Mehldau (3-4/95, Warner Bros 945997-2) CD
Melford	Myra	Even the Sounds Shine (5/94, hat ART 6161)
Melillo	Mike	Chet Baker: A Night at the Shalimar (5/87, Philology W59)CD
Melrose	Frank	Jelly Roll Stomp (1929, Bruns. 7062)Pianist & bandleader

Melvoin	Mike	H.Ellis & Ray Brown: Hot Tracks(1975, Conc.12)Pianist & organist
Mendez	Sergio	Sergio Mendez & Brazil 66-Look Around (AM, 1968)
Mendez	Eugenia	Afinidades (cdbaby.com)
Menefield	William	Big Will Leaps In (J Seven J7003) CD
Mengelberg	Misha	Driekusman, Total Loss (1964,1966, Varajazz 210)
Menzie	Beckie	Real Emotional Girl (cdbaby.com)
Meriwether	Roy	Soup & Onions/Soul Cookin' by The Roy Meriwether Trio (Columbia, CL-2433)
Merritt	Doris	Do What You Love (cdbaby.com)
Mesple	Taylor	Songs for Autumn (cdbaby.com)
Messina	Tony	T.M.Live (cdbaby.com)
Metz	Henrik	Henrik Metz (8/92, Music Mecca 1024-2) CD
Mickman	Herb	CD's w. Clayton-Hamilton Orch. (Capri; Conc.) Bassist, Pianist
Middleton	Rex	R.M. Hi-Fi'S-Orch.conducted by Buddy Bregman(Verve Clef,MGV-2035)LP
Migliazza	Arthur	Arthur Migliazza (cdbaby.com)
Mikami	Kuni	Lionel Hampton Orch. (April 1991); CD's: Time USA
Miles	Barry	Miles of Genius (1961, CP 804)
Miller	Max	Piano Moods, Columbia 10"
Miller	Mulgrew	Keys to the City (1985, Landmark 1507)

Miller	Sing	Old Times with S.M. (1975, Smoky Mary 1975S)
Miller	Vladimir	Frontiers (2/95, Leo LAB CD 0616) CD
Miller	Rod	R.M.Ragtime (cdbaby.com)
Miller	Dick	D.M.& Friends: Cape Song (cdbaby.com)
Miller	Harry	H.M. & The Satisfied Souls: Jazz Beauty Supply (cdbaby.com)
Million	Steve	Million to One (2/95, Palmetto PM-2014) CD
Millonzi	Ziggy	The Mil-Combo (Capitol, T-579)
Mills	Jess	J.M. & The Usual Suspects Jazz Combo:Right Out Of The Blue (cdbaby.com)
Milne	Andy	Ranee Lee-Jazz on Broadway (1992, Justin Time R2 79380)accompanist.
Mintel	Eric	E.M.Quartet: Hopscotch (cdbaby.com)
Mintun	Peter	Deep Purple and other Piano Solos from the 1920's and 1930's (cdbaby.com)
Misinterprotato		Now For The Free (cdbaby.com)
Mitchell	Dwike	Mitchell-Ruff Duo (1955, Epic 3221)
Mitchell	George	Ballads (cdbaby.com)
Mitchell	Rubin	Remarkable Rubin (Capitol, ST-2735)
Miwa	Yoko	In The Mist Of Time (cdbaby.com)
Mixon	Danny	Betty Carter: (1972, Bet-Car 1002)
Mlely	G.F.	Re-Entry (cdbaby.com)

Moer	Paul	Jack Montrose with Bob Gordon (1955, Atl. 1223)
Molinaro	Anthony	New Blue (cdbaby.com)
Monasterios	Sil Vano	Fostered (cdbaby.com)
Monk	Thelonious	T.M. (1954, Swing 33342)
Monroy	Sergio	Piano Flamenco (cdbaby.com)
Monteiro	Jeremy	My Foolish Heart (cdbaby.com)
Monteleone	Robert	Just Havin' Fun (cdbaby.com)
Montgomery	Buddy	B.M. at Maybeck-Volume 15-CCD4494
Montgomery	Little Brother	Vicksburg Blues (1930, Para. 13006)
Montoliu	Tete	The Music I Like to Play Vol.1-Tete Montoliu (Dec.1986, Soul Note, 121-180-1)
Moore	Alex	Alex Moore (July 30, 1960, Arthoolie LP, F-1008)
Moore	Gerry	Vic Lewis Jam Sessions:1945-The War Years(1945, Harl. 3009)
Moore	Dudley	D.M. Plays The Theme From Beyond The Fringe (1982, Atlantic, 1403)
Moran	Jason	Soundtrack To Human Motion (8/98, Blue Note 97431-2)CD
Moran	Jim	Out of Bounds (cdbaby.com)
Morgan	Ralph	Daily News Blues (cdbaby.com)
Morgan	Dick	Dick Morgan at The Showboat (Riverside, RLP-329)
Morgan	Loumell	Swingtime Jive (1941,1943, 1945, Stash, ST-108)

Moroni	Dado	D.M.Trio-Out of the Night (JFCD032) Jazz Focus CD
Morozumi	Hiro	Sharing (cdbaby.com)
Morreale	Pepe	Bobby Hacket Quartet: Easy Beat (Capitol)
Morris	Marlowe	Play the Thing (1961-2, Col. CS8619)
Morton	Jelly Roll	Smoke-house Blues(Beale Street Blues)(1926,Vic.20296)
Mosca	Sal	Sal Mosca For You (1979, Choice, CRS-1022)
Moss	Ed	Pam Ross & Ed Moss (cdbaby.com)
Moten	Bennie	Bennie Moten 1930-1932 (1930-32, Classics 591) CD
Motsinger	Buddy	Lois Boileau-I'll Be Around-The B.M. Trio('83,Courtney Rec.,CR112883)
Mseleku	Bheki	Meditations (1992, MCPS/Verve) Piano, Alto & Tenor Sax, Vocals
Muhler	Eric	E.M.Trio-Live at the Jazz School (cdbaby.com)
Munks	Tramane F.	Final Chapter (cdbaby.com)
Munn	Billy	St. Louis Blues (1949, Harmony A1008) Pianist & arranger
Munoz	Carli	Love Tales (cdbaby.com)
Muribus	George	Sam Most, But Beautiful (1976, Catalyst, CAT-7609)
Murphy	Rose	Women in Jazz- Pianists, Stash
Murphy	Greg	Orientation (cdbaby.com)
Musiker	Lee Elliott	CD's w. McCorkle (Concord); Soundtrack of W. Allen's "Crimes & Misdemeanors"

Mussolini	Romano	Topsy (1957, RCA LPM 10010)
Mustafa-Zade	Vagif	Jazz Compositions (1980, Mel. C601227780)
Myers	Amina Claudine	f- Songs for Mother E (1979, Leo 100)
Myers	Jason	Seems Like Old Times (cdbaby.com)
Myette	Willie	W.M.Trio- This is Jazz (cdbaby.com)
Nabatov	Simon	Tough Customer (1/92, Enja 7063-2) CD
Nam	John	Energy and Angular Momentum (cdbaby.com)
Nanton	Morris	Morris Nanton-Something We've Got (Prestige, PR-7409)
Napoleon	Marty	Blue Saxophones-Charlie Ventura and his orchestra (Norgran LP, MGN-1075)
Napoleon	Teddy	Leave us Leap/Dark Eyes(1945, Col.36802)
Nara	Haruko	My Favorite Things (1990, Jazz City) CD released?
Naura	Michael	Country Children (1977) Piano, Indian & Mexican Flutes, Composer
Navarro	Jorge	El loco son ustedes (CBS 8695)
Neeley	Jimmy	Misirlou-The Jimmy Neeley Trio (Tru-Sound, TRU-15002)
Negash	Elias	Peace (cdbaby.com)
Neloms	Bob	Pretty Music, India Navigation
Nelson	George	Beautiful Weekend (cdbaby.com)
Nelson	Matt	Something Crazy (cdbaby.com)

Nero	Peter	Peter Nero In Person (RCA, LPM-2710)
Neville	Chris	Songs We Like (cdbaby.com)
Newborn, Jr.	Phineas	Here Is Phineas-The Piano Artistry of Phineas Newborn Jr. (Atlantic, 1235)
Newton	David	D.N. Victim of Circumstance (1990, Linn AKH013)
Nicholas	Grant	Cherry Lane (cdbaby.com)
Nichols	Herbie	H.N. Trio (1955, BN 5068-9)
Nichols	Keith	I Like to Do Things For You (1991, Stomp Off)
Nighthawk	Frederick	Gathering Wave (cdbaby.com)
Nillson	Al	Smiling Skies (12/9/28- 402202-C- Okeh 41171)Side 65B-Franklin Mint Jazz
Nock	Mike	Climbing (1/79, Tomato 2696502)CD
Nordahl	Peter	Crazy She Calls Me (11/95, Sittel SITTEL SITCD 9232)CD
Norman	Cecil	Ragtime Piano Novelties of the Twenties (Folkways RBF 42)
Norman	Charlie	AFN-Boogie (1946, Col. DS1610, DS1687)Pianist & entertainer
Norris	Walter	W.N. at Maybeck-Volume 4, Concord,CCD4425
Novak	Larry	Buddy DeFranco: Chip off the Old Bop (1992, Concord Jazz, CCD4527)
Nurock	Kirk	CD's: Wergo; Adamo (composer & pianist)
Nye	Rick	R.N.-Highlights From The Third Annual Blues & Boogie Pno.Summit (cdbaby.com)
Oberhoff	Stephan	Conversations With My Father (cdbaby.com)

O'Brien	Hod	Opalessence (9/84, Criss Cross Criss 1012)
Occhipinti	Giorgio	The Kaos Legend (10/93,10/94, Leo LAB CD 012) CD
O'Connell	Bill	The Janet Lawson Quintet (1981, Inner City, IC 1116)LP
O'Farrill	Arturo Jr.	CD's: Mile; w. C. O' Farrill (Mile.)
O'Keefe	Jimmy	Ragtime Piano Interpretations (Folkways RF 24)
Oliveri	Edy	Chet Baker: Naima (6/83, 9/85, 11/87, Philology W52)CD
Olsen	Tom	Solo Piano (cdbaby.com)
Olson	Craig T.	Confessions of a Worshipper (cdbaby.com)
O'Neal	Johnny	Soulful Swinging (4/85, Just A Memory Records)CD
O'Neal	Brian	Mood Swings (cdbaby.com)
Onishi	Junko	Cruisin' (4/93, Blue Note 828447-2)CD
Opferkuch	John	The Kennedy Files (cdbaby.com)
O'Rourke	Brian	Ron Affif (Oct. 20-22, 1992, Pablo 2310949) CD
Orrje	Carl Fredrik	102 Greet St, NYC (5/96, Arietta ADCD 12)CD
Ortega	Frank	Twinkling Pinkies-Frank Ortega Trio (Jubilee, JLP-1051)
Otey	Lisa	Kitten On The Keys (cdbaby.com)
O'Toole	Knuckles	Honky Tonk Ragtime Piano (Grand Award, G.A.33-314)LP
Ovaciir		Ovaciir (cdbaby.com)

Overton	Hall	CD's w. Raney (Prest.)
Owen	Just	Hanging Out at Harv's Joint (cdbaby.com)
Ozer	Stephanie	O Comeco: New Beginnings in Brazillian Jazz (cdbaby.com)
Ozone	Makato	New York Now (1987, Columbia)
Pacheco	Marialy	M.P.Trio: Bendiciones (cdbaby.com)
Pacini	Tony	Piano a la carte (cdbaby.com)
Paguia	Marco	Marco Paguia Trio-Small Hours (cdbaby.com)
Paich	Marty	Mel Torme with the M.P. Dek-tette (1956, Beth.52)
Paige	Jewel	Jazz Women- A Feminist Retrospective, Stash
Palmieri	Eddie	Palmas (1993, Elektra Nonesuch)
Palmieri	Charlie	Impulsos (1975, Musical Productions)
Pancoast	Bob	Marv Meredith & his Orch.:Strings (and all that)Jazz(Strand SL1003)
Panich	Dimitry	One (cdbaby.com)
Papadimitriou	Sakis	Piano Plays (Leo LR 111)
Papirany	Dan	Session One (cdbaby.com)
Parham	Tiny	1926-1929 (Dec.1926 - July 22, 1929, Classics)
Paris	Norman	Love Songs for a Late Evening-Portia Nelson & the N.P.Trio, Columbia
Parker	Errol	A Night In Tunisia (4/91, Sahara 1015)CD

Parker	Johnny	Feline Stomp (1958, Sto. 366[EP])
Parker	Knocky	The Golden Treasury of Ragtime(c1968, Audiophile 89-92)
Parker	Sista Monica	Love, Soul & Spirit-Vol.1 (cdbaby.com)
Parlan	Horace	Musically yours (1979, Ste.1141)
Parmisano	Mario	Desde el Laberinto (cdbaby.com)
Parodi	Starr	Change (1991, Gift Horse)
Parrish	Avery	After Hours (1940, Bb 10879)
Particles	Charged	Sparks (cdbaby.com)
Partridge	John	Original Rags & Waltzes (cdbaby.com)
Pasqua	Alan	Dedications (12/95, Postcards POST 1012) CD
Paster	Bennett	B.P.,Gregory Ryan & Keith Hall-Skyline (cdbaby.com)
Patin	Bob	In A Mind's Eye (cdbaby.com)
Patterson	Don	o- Four Dimensions (1967, Prst. 7533)
Patton	Big John	The Way I Feel (1964, BN 84174) Organist
Patton	Jeb	A Lovesome Thing (cdbaby.com)
Pauer	Fritz	F.P. Trio (1970, MPS 15268)
Paul	David	Interpretations (cdbaby.com)
Payne	Bennie	Ebb Tide (1937, Var. 657) Pianist & singer

Pearce	Jim	Thirty Year Waltz (cdbaby.com)
Pearson	Duke	It Could only Happen to you (1970, BN LA317)
Pearson	Gay	Nature Girl (GP Records)CD
Pecuna	Buca	B.P.:The Picture Player (cdbaby.com)
Pedersen	John	Paradise (cdbaby.com)
Peet	Wayne	Down-in Ness (9/81, Nine Winds NW0111)
Peiffer	Bernard	B.P. & His Jazz Piano Plays Prelude,Fugue & Trio On Lullaby of Birdland,IP
Perciful	Jack	Harry James Septet (1964, MGM 4274)
Perez	Danilo	Jeanie Bryson-Tonight I Need You So(1994, Telarc CD83348)CD
Perez	Oscar	Nuevo Comienzo (cdbaby.com)
Perkins	Carl	Introducing C.P., 1956, Dootone 211)
Perrella	Harry	Ragtime Piano Interpretations (Folkways RF 24)
Perry	Sacha	Eretik (cdbaby.com)
Persiany	Andre	Swinging Here and There (1956-8, Pathe 05411721)
Peterson	Jean Arland	Wish (Celebration)
Peterson	Oscar	The President Plays with The Oscar Peterson Trio (Norgran LP,MGN-1054)
Peterson	Jeanne Arland	Timeless (cdbaby.com)
Peterson	Bill	Mariah Picot with the B.P.Trio-Notes on the Bridge (cdbaby.com)

Petrescu	Marian	Marian Petrescu-Pianist (June 16 & 17, 1986, Kompass, KOLP-74)
Petrides	Matt	Skies of Blue (cdbaby.com)
Petrin	Umberto	Ooze (4-5/92, Splasc(h) CDH 384.2) CD
Petrucciani	Michel	Michel Petruciani (April 3-4, 1981, Owl)
Pfeffer	Adam	Piano Puss (cdbaby.com)
Pfister	Stephen	Cold Hands, Warm Heart (cdbaby.com)
Philippe	Claude	Finally, Celebration
Phillips	Sonny	I Concentrate on You (1977, Muse 5157)Organist & pianist
Pichon	Fats	Doggin' That Thing/Yo Yo (1929, Vic. 38544)Pianist ,singer,arranger
Pickens	Harry	Passionate Ballads (2/98, Double-Time DTRCD-146)CD
Pickens	Willie	It`s About Time, Southpart
Pieranunzi	Enrico	E.P. Featuring Art Farmer (1981, ISIS 121021-2)CD
Pierce	Billy	New Orleans: The Living Legends (1961, OBC) CD
Pierce	Nat	Juggernaut Strikes Again(1981, Conc.183)
Pierce	Jim	Washington Square Park (cdbaby.com)
Pierson	Tom	Unchained Melody (cdbaby.com)
Piket	Roberta	Unbroken Line (4/96, Criss Cross CRISS 1140)CD
Pintchik	Leslie	So Glad To Be Here (cdbaby.com)

Piscione	Randy	Hymns For Him (cdbaby.com)
Pistorius	Steve	Kiss Me Sweet (7/90, Stomp Off CD-1221) CD-Pianist & Vocal
Pitson	Jeff	Invisible Love (cdbaby.com)
Pitts	Trudy	Me, Myself & I (cdbaby.com)
Pizzurro	Teresa	Shades of Piano (cdbaby.com)
Plaks	Eric	E.P.Five-Rooftoop Reveries (cdbaby.com)
Plimey	Paul	Both Sides Of The Same Mirror (11/89, Nine Winds 0135)CD
Pohjola	Mika	On The Move (11/96, MikaMusik MMK97)CD
Poladian	Patrick	Comfort Me Blue (cdbaby.com)
Polito	John	Crossing the Line (cdbaby.com)
Pollard	Terry (Jean)	Terry Gibbs Quartet (1953,Bruns. BL58055)Pianist & vibraphonist
Pollock	Muriel	Ragtime Piano Interpretations (Folkways RF 24)
Pompe	Marc	Nobody Else But Me (cdbaby.com)
Porter	Randy	Eight Little Feet (cdbaby.com)
Portmann	Mark	Westside (cdbaby.com)
Potts	Bill	Lester Young in Wash.,DC(PL2308219,2308225,2308228,2308230),arrang.
Powell	Richie	More of Johnny Hodges (1951-4, Norg.1009)
Powell	Dee	Saturday Night Live At The Arlington Hotel With The Reggie (Arlington)

Powell	Bud	Piano Interpretations by Bud Powell (Verve,D. S.Martin cover, UMV-2573)
Powell	Mel	Mel Powell Out on a Limb (Vanguard, VRS-8506)
Powers	Dave	Listen to This (cdbaby.com)
Prawdzik	Charlie	Dreamworld (cdbaby.com)
Prather	Sam	Split Personalities (cdbaby.com)
Press	Ralph	The Great American Ragtime Revival (cdbaby.com)
Previn	Andre	Andre Previn's Trio-King Size! (Nov.1958, M-3570)
Price	Sammy	Sweet Subsitute (Nov. 1, 1979, Sackville)
Priest	David	Smile (cdbaby.com)
Priestley	Brian	You Taught My Heart to Sing (1994, Spirit of Jazz) Piano, Arranger, Writer
Prince	Mary Lou	Armchair Magician (cdbaby.com)
Profit	Clarence	Times Square Blues/Hot and Bothered, 1940, Decca 8503)
Prude	Terrell	T.N.T. (cdbaby.com)
Pryor	Lorenzo	1700 Miles from St.Louis (cdbaby.com)
Pullen	Don	f- Solo Piano Album (1975, Sack.3008)
Punch	Sweet	Magic Stones (cdbaby.com)
Purbrook	Colin	Shades of Blue with Don Rendell & Ian Carr(1964, Col.SX1733)
Purnell	Alton	A.P.Quartet (1958, WB 1228)Pianist & singer

Pyne	Mike	Alone Together (1977, Spot. 506) Pianist & cornet
Queener	Charlie	Southern Comfort/Gotta Be This or That (1945, Musi. 328)
Queensland	Jazz	J.Q. and Vol.2- The Merlo Collection (cdbaby.com)
Quelar	Liz	L.Q. & Seth Farber- The Other Side (cdbaby.com)
Quesnell	Roger	A Passion For Hymns (cdbaby.com)
Ra	Sun	Angels and Demons at Play (1955-7, Saturn 407)
Race	Steve	Take One (1965, World Record Club 453)Pianist,arranger,broadcaster
Rachel	Z	w. Shorter (Verve)
Ragas	Henry	Original Dixieland Jazz Band:Bluin' The Blues(1918, Vic.18483)
Ramchandran	Sameer	S.R.Trio:Roundabout (cdbaby.com)
Ramirez	Ram	Rampart Ram (1973-4, MJR 8122)
Randall	Chico	Relaxin' with Chica Randall (1958, Roulette, SR25092)LP
Randall	Mark	M.R.- at the Cafe Royal (Mirth)
Randalu	Kristjan	Tidbits (cdbaby.com)
Randi	Don	The Don Randi Trio-Where Do We Go From Here? (1962, Verve, V6-8469)
Ranier	Tom	CD's: Jackson, Johnson & Co. (Pab.)
Raphael	Lenore	Reflections (cdbaby.com)
Rashid	Steve	As In A Mirror (cdbaby.com)

Raskin	Milt	Well, Git it (1942, Vic.27887)
Ray	Matt	We Got It (cdbaby.com)
Rea	Danilo	CD's: C. Fuller-Roma Trio (Timel.)
Reale	Michael F.	Embracing Change (cdbaby.com)
Rebello	Jason	Clearer View (1991, Novus 63000)
Rebic	Don	Lainie Kazan-Body & Soul(1995, Music Masters 0612-65126-2)CD accom.
Rebillot	Pat(rick)	Free Fall (1973, Atl. 1663)
Red	Piano	Atlanta Bounce (1993, Arhoolie) Blues singer & pianist (is he Speckled Red?)
Red	Speckled	Boogie Woogie: Great Original Performances ('28-41, RPCD601)1 track on CD
Redd	Freddie	F.R. Trio (1955, Prst. 197)
Reed	Eric	Soldier's Hymn (11/90, Candid CCD 79511)CD
Reichel	Fritz Shulz	Crazy Otto-Honky Tonk Piano (Decca, DL 8737)LP
Reilly	Jack	Live In Poland (cdbaby.com)
Reilly	Jack	The Most Minor-The John LaPorta Quartet (Everest, LPBR-5037)
Reinherz	Sid	Ragtime Piano Novelties of the Twenties (Folkways RBF 42)
Rejman	Andrew	Silent Sun (cdbaby.com)
Renaud	Henri	H.R.-Al Cohn Quartet (1954, Swing 33332)
Renzi	Mike	Anne Marie Moss: Don't You Know Me? (1981, Stash ST211)

Report	Minority	Classified (cdbaby.com)
Revray		Sophisticated Sounds (cdbaby.com)
Reynolds	Jimmy	Henry "Red"Allen:Nothing's Blue But The Sky(1936, Voc.3245)Pno.&Bandldr.
Rhodes	Todd	Red Boy at the Mardi Gras (1949, Sensation 15)Pianist & Arranger
Ricchiutti	Mike	The Way I See It (cdbaby.com)
Rich	Fred	Till We Meet Again (1940, Voc.5507)Pianist & bandleader
Richard	Matt	Jim Robitaille: The Art of the Duo (cdbaby.com)
Richards	Red	Soft Buns (1978, West 54 8000)
Richards	Tim	On The Level (1994, 33 Records)
Richards	Grant	Extra Step (cdbaby.com)
Richardson	Kip	Showers In Their Season (cdbaby.com)
Richey	Garon	Tablets of My Heart (cdbaby.com)
Ridl	Jim	Pat Martino-Interchange (1994, Muse MCD 5529)CD
Riggins	Emmanuel	Seasons (cdbaby.com)
Riley	Howard	Intertwine (1975,Mosaic 771)
Riley	Doug	D.R. with Tyler Yarema & John Roby-Stride(3 pianists)(cdbaby.com)
Risby	Bill	Looking Up (cdbaby.com)
Ritz	Beverly	Beverly Ritz:Tango, Where Did The Time Go? (cdbaby.com)

Rivera	Dave	Don Byas/Savoy Jam Party (8/31/44, Savoy SJL 2213)
Roberts	David Thomas	Folk Ragtime: 1899-1914 (94-96, Stomp Off 1317)CD
Roberts	Jim	Brian Torff- Manhattan Hoedown, Audiophile
Roberts	Judy	Trio (1985, Pausa)
Roberts	Luckey	Luckey Roberts & The Lion- Harlem Piano, Good Time Jazz
Roberts	Jim	Somewhere in Time (cdbaby.com)
Roberts	Marcus	Alone with Three Giants (Jun.3-Sep.22,1990, Novus 3051)
Robertson	Raf	Universal Rhythm (cdbaby.com)
Robichaux	Joseph	The Riff (1933, Voc. 2592)
Robinson	Chris	The C.R.Trio-"Live at the Corner" (cdbaby.com)
Robinson	J(oseph)	Duos with L. Hegamin:Down Hearted Blues/Wanna Go South Again Blues 1923)
Robinson	Reginald	Sounds in Silhouette (1994, Delmark DE-670) CD
Robinson	Doug	Jazzoo/D.R.-Two Days in November (cdbaby.com)
Robinson	Peter	P.R.Group- Hideaway (cdbaby.com)
Robison	Willard	Ragtime Piano Novelties of the Twenties (Folkways RBF 42)
Rocco	Maurice	LP's: Dec; Vict.
Rodgers	Gene	G.R./Slam Stewart/Jo Jones (1972, BB 33047)
Rodriguez	Rod	How Come You Do Me Like You Do?(1933, Decca F3972)w/Spike Hughes'Orch

Rodriguez	Bob	Mist ('94, Nine Winds NWCD 0177)CD
Rodriguez	Nicholas	Sweet Sue, Just You(5/18/33-13356-A, Decca F3972) 75A-Franklin Mint Jazz
Rodriguez	Anthony	A.R. & Poetology (cdbaby.com)
Roe	Rick	The Changeover (cdbaby.com)
Rogers	Milt	Rogers With Heart Plays Rodgers & Heart (Dot, DLP3055)LP
Rogers	Billy	Never Alone (cdbaby.com)
Rohde	Bryce	Corners (1963, CBS BP233046)
Rolando	Dean	Laurel Masse-Alone Together (1984, PAUSA, PR-7165)LP
Roscoe	Glenn	From The Heart (cdbaby.com)
Rose	Wally	W.R. on Piano(1970, Blackbird 12007)
Rosenthal	Ted	At Maybeck Recital Hall Vol. 38 (10/94, Concord CCD 4648) CD
Rosewoman	Michele	Contrast High (July 1988, Enja 79607)
Rosnes	Renee	R.R. (April 18, 1988-Feb. 4, 1989, Blue Note 93561)
Ross	Arnold	The A.R. Trio- Barbed Wire,Bunns & Beans, Jazz Chronicles
Ross	Florian	Seasons And Places (3/98, Naxos Jazz 86029-2)CD
Ross	Ron	Ragtime Renaissance (cdbaby.com)
Ross	Steve	Flying Colors (cdbaby.com)
Rossborough	Patricia	Ragtime Piano Novelties of the Twenties(Folkways RBF 42)

Rowe	Jay	Red, Hot and Smooth (cdbaby.com)
Rowland	Jess	h.29 (cdbaby.com)
Rowland	Billy	Bill Rowland Plays Boogie Woogie (Grand Award, GA-259-SD)
Rowles	Jimmy	J.R.& Ray Brown-As Good as it Gets,
Roy	Teddy	CD's w. Eddie Edwards & ODJB in "The Commodore Story" (Story.)
Rubalcaba	Gonzalo	The Blessing (5/91, Blue Note CDP 7971972)CD
Rubardt	Steve	Homemade (cdbaby.com)
Rubin	Gideon	The American Sound (cdbaby.com)
Rubyana		Saint Joan d'arc(piano score) (cdbaby.com)
Rucker	Ellyn	This Heart of Mine (1989, Capri)
Ruiz	Hilton	H.R. Trio- Live at Jazz Unite, Jazz Unite
Rundqvist	Gosta	Until We Have Faces (5/94, Sittel SITCD 9212) CD
Rushen	Patrice	Prelusion (1974, Prst. 10089)
Russell	George	The Jazz Workshop (1956, RCA LPM1372)
Russell	Luis	Luis Russell & His Orchestra (1/29-8/34, Topaz TPZ 1039) CD
Russell	J.L.	Soul of a Poet (cdbaby.com)
Ryza	Mike	The M.R.Trio: Full of Ideas (cdbaby.com)
Sabatini	Stefano	Wonderland (4/91, Splasc(h) H 360-2) CD

Sabatino	Paolo Di	Introducing P.D.S. (cdbaby.com)
Sagebin	Glauco	When Baden Meets Trane (cdbaby.com)
Saisse	Philippe	Storyteller (cdbaby.com)
Salvador	Emiliano	Ayer y Hoy(Qbadisc QB9011)
Salvatore	Sergio	Tune Up (1994, GRP GRD-9762)
Sam	Detroit	Detroit Sam (cdbaby.com)
Sample	Joe	The Three (Nov.1975, Inner City, IC-6007)
Samuels	Jerry	Samuels & Wesar Perform the Music of Clare Fischer (cdbaby.com)
Sanders	Joe	Deep Henderson (1926, Vic. 20081)Pianist,singer,bandleader
Sands	Christian	Foot Prints (cdbaby.com)
Sannes	Eivin	Sandu (5/90, Gemini GMCD 67) CD
Santisi	Ray	Spellbinder (cdbaby.com)
Sardaby	Michael	M.S. in New York (1972, Debs 540)
Sarmanto	Heikki	Suomi (1983)
Satoh	Masahiko	Amphorphism (1985, Portrait, OR44194)LP
Satyan	Arthur	Art For Art's Sake (cdbaby.com)
Sauls	Noreen	Generation (1985, Muse)
Saunders	Keith	CD's w. Hardbop (TCB)

Saussy	Tupper	Discover Tupper Saussy (Monument , MLP 8004)
Savage	Matt	The M.S. Trio: Cutting Loose (cdbaby.com)
Savery	Finn	Many Moments (1982, Met. 15818) Pianist & composer
Savolainen	Jarmo	Solo Duo Trio (cdbaby.com)
Saye	Joe	A Wee Bit of Jazz-Joe Saye and his piano (May 1957, SR-60052)
Scaggiari	Stefan	Stefanitely (4/93, Concord CCD 4570) CD
Scaletta	Don	The Don Scaletta Trio-All In Good Time! (Capitol, T-2328)
Schaefer	Hal	The Extraordinary Jazz Pianist (1976, Discovery DS781)
Schaefer	Ed	Outland (cdbaby.com)
Schell	Gaea	Dream Away (cdbaby.com)
Schell	Jack	Ageless Music (cdbaby.com)
Schiff	Bobby	Late Game (cdbaby.com)
Schifrin	Lalo	L.S. (1962, Roul. 52088) Composer & pianist
Schlippenbach	Alexander von	f-Piano Solo (1977, FMP430)
Schmeling	Paul	Dick Johnson-Swing Shift (March 1981, Concord, CJ-167)
Schneider	Maria	Evanescence (1993, Enja) Arranger, Piano
Schneiderman	Rob	New Outlook (1/88, Reservoir RSR 106)CD
Schoberg	Paul	Sunrise (cdbaby.com)

Schoebel	Elmer	Copenhagen/ Prince of Wails(1929, Bruns. 4652)Arranger,composer,pianist
Schroder	Karl	Farm Girl Blues (cdbaby.com)
Schroeder	Gene	Liza/ I ain't got nobody (1944, Black & White 33)
Schroeter	Guilherme	Paisagem (landscape) (cdbaby.com)
Schutt	Arthur	Charleston Chasers:Farewell Blues('27, Col.1539D) Pianist,arranger,composer
Schweizer	Irene	Hexensabbat (1977, FMP 0500)
Schwendener	Ben	B.S. & Marc Rossi: Living Geometry (cdbaby.com)
Scott	Dred	Eight (+3) Tristano Compositions'89-for W. Marsh Braxton('89, hatart CD6052)
Scott	Hazel	Hazel's Boogie Woogie(1942, Decca 18340)
Scott	Shirley	Great Scott! (1958, Prst. 7143)
Scott	Stephen	Aminah's Dream (10/92, Verve 517 996) CD
Scott	Rusty	The R.S.Quartet: Short Bread (cdbaby.com)
Scott	Percy	P.S.A Nice Day in Paris (cdbaby.com)
Scott	Bar	The Woodstock Cycle (cdbaby.com)
Scott	Bobby	The Gene Krupa Quartet (Cleff, MG C-668)
Seales	Marc.	CD's w. New Stories (Origin)
Sealy	Joe	J.S. Trio- Clear Vision, Sackville
Sean		Singers ruin perfectly good bands (cdbaby.com)

Sedergreen	Bob	The Ted Vining Trio Live at PBS-FM (1981, Jazznote 029)
Seits	Marilyn	Tribute (cdbaby.com)
Selby	Kevin B.	At My Father's Cabin (cdbaby.com)
Sellani	Renato	Chet Baker In Milan(9/10/59, OJC 370)CD
Senensky	Bernie	Homeland (1/91, Timeless SJP 426)CD
Shalom	Sasi	Long-Time Coming (cdbaby.com)
Shane	Mark	CD's: M. Grosz (J & M); appears on film soundtrack of "The Cotton Club"
Shannon	Terry	A Tribute to Tubbs (1963, Spot. SPJ 902)
Sharon	Ralph	The R.S. Trio (1956, Beth. 41)
Sharp	A	Sunset Blue (uncut) (cdbaby.com)
Shaw	Lee	L.S. OK! (1983, Cadence)
Shea	Michael	Last Night While You Slept (6/93, Accurate AC-5007) CD
Shearing	George	A Shearing Caravan-The George Shearing Quintet (MGM, E-3175)
Sheldon	Nina	Secret Places (1987, Plug Records)
Sherman	Daryl	I've Got My Fingers Crossed (1990's, Audiophile)
Sherman	Jimmy	A Sailboat in the Moonlight (1937, Voc.3605)
Sherman	Ray	CD's w. Jack Sheldon (Conc.)
Sherrod	James B.	Take Me To The Park (cdbaby.com)

Shifrin	Eric	Eric & The Incrowd (cdbaby.com)
Shilansky	Mark	Different Songs (cdbaby.com)
Shipp	Matthew	Points (1990, Silkheart SHCD 129)CD
Shirley	Don	The Don Shirley Point of View (1972, Atlantic, SD-1605)
Shook	Travis	Travis Shook (1993, Columbia CK 53138/473770-2) CD
Short	Bobby	Bobby Short Live at the Cafe Carlye (Dec.1973, 2LP's, SD-2-609)
Shouse	Daniel	Daniel (cdbaby.com)
Shreve	Dick	Jazz Montage (Liberty LRP 3292)
Sibirsky	Charles	C.B./Murray Wall- Just Jazz, Just Two (cdbaby.com)
Sidran	Ben	Have You Met ...Barcelona? (10/87, Orange Blue OB 002)CD
Siebert	Bob	My Bohemian Legacy (cdbaby.com)
Siegel	Al	Ragtime Piano Novelties of the Twenties (Folkways RBF 42)
Sifter	Suzanna	Awakening (cdbaby.com)
Signorelli	Frank	St. Louis Hop/ A Blues Serenade (1926, PAct 36535)
Silver	Trudy	Heroes, Heroines (1987, Under Open Sky)
Silver	Horace	Art Blakey w/ The Original Jazz Messengers('56,Columbia Odyssey, 32160246)
Silverman	Robert	Light on Water (cdbaby.com)
Silverstein	Herb	H.S.,Richard Drexler & Friends-Beach Walker (cdbaby.com)

Simas	Luiz	New Chorinhos from Brazil (cdbaby.com)
Simmerman	Scott	Notes That Rhyme (cdbaby.com)
Simmons	Art	Don Byas on Blue Star (July 4,1950, Emarcy 833405-2) CD
Simmons	Norman	N.S.Trio (1956, Argo 607)
Simmons	Christopher	Solo Piano: Piece, Time, With Peace (cdbaby.com)
Simon	Alan	Rainsplash (5/83-8/84, Cadence CJR 1027)
Simon	Ed	CD: Eubanks (GRP)
Simon	Alan	The Present (cdbaby.com)
Simon	Edward	Edward Simon (cdbaby.com)
Simone	Nina	N.S. Sings Billy Holiday-Lady Sings the Blues, Strand
Simpson	Cassino	Little Willie Blues (1929, Bruns. 7058)
Singleton	Jonathan	Soul Food (cdbaby.com)
Siregar	Rhesa	Spiritual (cdbaby.com)
Sjosten	Lars	Bells, Blues And Brotherhood (5-12/81, Dragon DRLP 46)
Slack	Freddie	CowCow Boogie (1942, Cap. 102)
Slim	Memphis	Chicago Piano (1951-58, Paula 015)
Slinger	Cees	Sling Shot (4/85, Timeless SJP 225) CD
Smalls	Cliff	Swing and Things (1976. MJR 8131)

Smith	Fred	Music del Rey (cdbaby.com)
Smith	Howard	Tommy Dorsey: Boogie Woogie (1938, Vic. 26054)
Smith	Huey "Piano"	Pitta Pattin' (1987, Charly)
Smith	Jimmy	o- The Sermon (1957-8, BN 4011)
Smith	Johnny "Hammond"	o- Stimulation (Prestige)
Smith	Leonard	W/ Ford Dabney-Castle House Rag(2/10/14, 14433-2 Vict.55372) 53B-F.MintJazz
Smith	Lonnie	o-Expansions (1975, FD 10934)
Smith	Michael	Austin Stream (1976, FMP SAJ09)Keyboard player,composer, leader
Smith	Pine Top	Pine Top's Boogie Woogie/Pine Top's Blues(1928,Voc.1245)
Smith	Willie "the Lion"	Reminiscing the Piano Greats (1950, Vogue LD008)oral history
Smith	Tyrone Marquis	The 5th Seal "Here" (cdbaby.com)
Smith	Demorris	Jazzy Me! (cdbaby.com)
Smith	Derek	Derek Smith Trio-Dark Eyes (June 1983, Eastwind, EWIND-711)
Smith	Paul	Intensive Care-Louie Bellson -Ray Brown-P.S. (March 1978, PAUSA, PR-7167)
Smythe	Pat(rick)	Personal Portrait (1967, Col. SCX6249)
Snow	Thomas	Northern Standard Time (cdbaby.com)
Snyder	Bill	Sweet and Lovely-Bill Snyder at the Piano (Decca, DL-8469)
Soko		In November Sunlight (cdbaby.com)

Solal	Martial	Martial Solal (Capitol, T-10261)
Sonstevold	Gunnar	You Got Me Woodooed/It Happened in Kaloha (1940, Col. DS 1219)
Soper	Tut	For No Reason At All In C (Dec.1957-Empirical 1076) 68A-Franklin Mint Jazz
Sorrells	Mark	December Night (cdbaby.com)
Soskin	Mark	View From Here (7/30/31,92, Bellaphon 126, Paddle Wheel 126)
Sote		Celebrating the Gift (cdbaby.com)
South	Harry	Sound Venture (1966, EMI SX6076) Pianist,arranger,composer
Souza	Heidi Eger	Souza Plays Joplin (cdbaby.com)
Sowash	Bradley	Bittersweet (cdbaby.com)
Spann	Otis	The Blues of Otis Spann Plus (1964, See For Miles 389)
Spendel	Christoph	Ready For Take-Off (9/88, L+R 45010)CD
Spivey	Victoria	The Queen and Her Knights (1965, Spivey 1006)Singer & pianist
Springer	Joe	Buddy Rich: That Drummer's Band (1942, Col. 36819)
Spurr	Ken	Sometime Ago (cdbaby.com)
Stacy	Jess	Stacy Still Swings (1974, Chi.133)
Staffard	Abebi	Mr.B (cdbaby.com)
Stark	Michael	In Mind (cdbaby.com)
Steele	Joe	Top and Bottom (1929, Vic. 38066)

Steele	Squeek	Ragtime Volume One (cdbaby.com)
Steger	Elliot	Making Time (cdbaby.com)
Stein	Helmut	The H.S. Experience- Uptown Game(cdbaby.com)
Stein	Lou	Honky Tonk Piano featuring Lou Stein (Mercury LP, MG-20159)
Stenson	Bobo	Dansere (1975, ECM 1075)
Stepp	Rodney	R.S. & B.S.B: Steppin' Out (cdbaby.com)
Stern	Peggy	Lunasea (1992, Soul Note with Lee Konitz)
Sternberg	Steve	Shout For Joy (cdbaby.com)
Stetch	John	Greengrove (Justin Time JTR 8473-2) CD
Stevens	Michael Jefry	Elements (3/94, Leo CD LR241)CD
Stewart	Jeff	Classic Stew (cdbaby.com)
Stiles	Joan	Love Call (cdbaby.com)
Stitzel	Mel	New Orleans Rhythm Kings: Maple Leaf Rag(1923, Gen. 5104)
Stoler	David	Urband Legends (cdbaby.com)
Stoller	Bruce	On the Loose (cdbaby.com)
Stone	Jesse	Snaky Feelings (1937, Var. 521) Pianist & arranger
Stone	Sparrow	Queen For A Day (cdbaby.com)
Story	Liz	Unaccountable Effect, Windham Hill

Stout	Geanie	Geanie Stout (cdbaby.com)
Strandberg	Goran	Ringvida (5/85, Dragon DRLP 105)
Strayhorn	Billy	B.S. Trio (1950, Mercer 1001)
Strazzeri	Frank	Relaxin' (1982, Seabreeze 1007)
Strickland	Mike	My Favorite Things (1994, MSP 5153) CD
Strinnholm	Jan.	Strinnholm-95 (3/95, Sittel SITCD 9224)CD
Stritch	Billy	Billy Stritch (1991, DRG Records)
Strock	Doug	Piano Dreams (cdbaby.com)
Stuart	Kirk	Sarah Vaughan: Sassy Swings The Tivoli (1963, Merc. 60831)
Sturm	Fred	American Rags, Brazilian Tangos, Afrocuban Dances (cdbaby.com)
Sukman	Harry	Command Performance-The Piano & Orch.of Harry Sukman(Liberty, LRP-3135)
Sullivan	Frank	Live! (cdbaby.com)
Sullivan	Katie	Lucky Number 7 (cdbaby.com)
Sullivan	Joe	New Solos by an Old Master-Joe Sullivan (1953, Riverside, RLP-12-202)
Sunstrom	Tim	Inasmuch (cdbaby.com)
Surace	Ron	Bobby Brack Trio, Kent State Jazz Date (Colpix, CP-405)
Surflounge.com		Surflounge, com: Surf Lounge Blues (cdbaby.com)
Sutton	Ralph	Jazz At The Olympics-The Ralph Sutton Quartet (Jan.1960, Omega, OSL-51)

Svensson	Esbjorn	Mr And Mrs Handkerchief (3/95, Prophone PCD 028) CD
Svensson	Reinhold	Mainstream Jazz Piano-John Evans-Reinhold Svensson (Omega, OSL-49)
Swanerud	Thore	More Than You Know (10-12/84, Dragon DRLP 85)
Swann	Bill	Three (cdbaby.com)
Swanson	David	Dinner at Eight Vol.1 (cdbaby.com)
Swift	Duncan	The Broadwood Concert (1990, Big Bear BEARCD 34)CD
Sykes	Roosevelt	The Return of R.S.(Prestige/Bluesville 1006)vocals & pianist
Syran	George	(Pres. 7033)
Szabados	Gyorgy	Szabraxtondos (1984, Krem 17909) Pianist,composer,arranger
Szakcsi	Sa-chi	Straight Ahead (1994, GRP GRD-9737)
Taborn	Craig	Light Made Lighter (Oct.23, 2001, Thirsty Ear)
Takase	Aki	Blue Monk (1991, Enja)
Takenaka	Makoto	Mio (cdbaby.com)
Talbert	Tom	Duke's Domain (10/91-5/93, Sea Breeze CDSB-2058) CD
Talia		My Notes (cdbaby.com)
Talaga	Steve	Two Worlds (cdbaby.com)
Tamer		Beginning To See The Light (cdbaby.com)
Tanksley	Francesca	Live on Tour in the Far East (Steeplechase, Vol.1)

Tannebring	Bill	B.T. Live in Laguna (cdbaby.com)
Tapscott	Horace	The Call (1979, Nimbus 246)
Tatum	Art	The Art of Tatum-Piano Solos (Decca, DL-8715)
Taylor	Cecil	Silent Tongues (1974, Ari. 1005)
Taylor	John	Decipher (1973, MPS 2121290)
Taylor	Mike	The M.T. Trio (1966, Col. SX6137)
Taylor	Sandy	Carol Kidd (1984, Aloi, AKH 003)LP
Taylor	Gregory	In The Flow (cdbaby.com)
Taylor	Dave	Big Band Boogie & Jive (cdbaby.com)
Taylor	Billy	Evergreens-Billy Taylor (ABC-Paramount, ABC-112)
Teagarden	Norma	J.Teagarden: The Swingin' Gate, Giants of Jazz 1026
Tee	Richard	The Bottom Line (1985, EB6364)
Teitelbaum	Richard	s- Homage to Charles Parker (1979, BS 0029)
Templeton	Alec	Andre Kostelantz & Orch.-Rhapsody in Blue, Columbia
Tennyson	John Gentry	Real World Trio (cdbaby.com)
Tepfer	Dan	D.T.Trio- Before The Storm (cdbaby.com)
Terrason	Jacky	What's New (7/16-18, 1992, Jazz Aux Remparts 64003)
Texada	Clarence "Tex"	Curiosity (cdbaby.com)

Theurer	Martin	Moon Mood (7/79, FMP 0700)
Thibaudet	Jean-Yves	Conversations with Bill Evans (July 26-29, 1996-London)CD
Thomas	Ron	17 Solo Piano Improvisations (cdbaby.com)
Thomas	Matt	The M.T. Project (cdbaby.com)
Thomas	Robert	View From the Parkway (cdbaby.com)
Thompson	Eddie	When Lights Are Low (1980, HEP 2007)
Thompson	Sir Charles	Hey, there! (1974, BB 33071)
Thompson	Butch	The Butch Thompson Trio Plays Favorites (Mar.16-17, 1992, Solo Art)
Thompson	Raleigh	Make Believe (cdbaby.com)
Thompson	Jeter	Sky High-The Quartette Tres Bien (Decca, DL-4715)
Thompson, Jr.	Alan	Flight of Hands (cdbaby.com)
Thorn	Stan	In a Curious Way (cdbaby.com)
Thorne	Francis	Piano Improvisations-Francis Thorne (Owl Records, ORLP-5)LP
Thornhill	Claude	C.T.- A Memory of Claude, Monmouth Evergreen
Threemonks		Threemonks: Spirit-That-Moves-In-All-Things (cdbaby.com)
Tillman	Eric	A Beautiful World (cdbaby.com)
Timmons	Bobby	From The Bottom (1964, Riverside)
Tippett	Keith	Mujician (1981, FMP SAJ37)

Toabe	Bob	Hope and Comfort (cdbaby.com)
Todd	Tommy	Caravan (1946- 112:Encore 510)Side 75A-Franklin Mint Jazz
Tommasi	Amadeo	Chet Baker: The Italian Sessions(1962, RCA Bluebird 82001)CD
Tompkins	Ross	A Pair To Draw To-Herb Ellis and Ross Tompkins (1976, Concord, CJ-17)
Tonolo	Marcello	D.O.C. (7/86, Splasc(h) H 119)
Tonooka	Sumi	With an Open Heart, Radiant
Toolajian	Loren	Into The Light (cdbaby.com)
Torregano	Michael	Without Your Love (cdbaby.com)
Torres	Nestor R.	Don Nestor (cdbaby.com)
Tosti	Bendi	Solo Jazz Piano-Vol.1 (cdbaby.com)
Towns	Colin	Still Life (1998, Provocateur PVC 1015)CD-Keyboards, Arranger
Townsend	Bross	CD's: Claves; w. D. Staton (Muse)
Tracey	Stan	on Stan Tracey....in Person (1966, Col.SX6124)
Tradewinds		Tradewinds (cdbaby.com)
Trenner	Don	Les Brown Concert Modern (Capitol LP,T-959)
Triglia	William	Hank D'Amico (1954, Beth. 1006)
Trio	Cascade Jazz	Cascade Jazz Trio: Valley Breezes (cdbaby.com)
Trippel	Fritz	Whisky Time (1964, Phi. 625101)

Tristano	Lennie	Lennie Tristano-Requiem (Atlantic 2 LP's, SD-2-7003)
Troncoso	David	Meant to Be (Dii Records-D2-001)
Trotter	Terry	CD's: Mama; w. Jim Self (d'Note)
Troup	Bobby	Voc. & Pianist-LP (VSOP); CD (Star Line)
Trovajoli	Armando	Pick Yourself Up! (1959, RCA LPM 10019)
Troy	Hank	Never Really Silent (cdbaby.com)
Trythall	Richard	Jelly Roll Morton Piano Music (cdbaby.com)
Trzaskowski	Andrzej	Polish Jazz: Vol.2 -A.T.('65-66,Polskie Nagrania MUZAPNCD052)CD
Tsukahara	Kotaro	CD's w. Milt Jackson (available in Japan)
Tucker	Bobby	Billy Holiday: I Thought About You (1954, Clef 89150)
Tucker	Mickey	Jazz on a Sunday Afternoon-Vol.III (April 1973, Accord, SN-7163)
Turner	Raymond	Ragtime Piano Interpretations (Folkways RF 24)
Turner	Sean	Begin Again (cdbaby.com)
Turner	Joe	Joe Turner-King of Stride (Chiaroscuro, CR-147)
Twardzik	Richard	Chet Baker-Rondette (1955, Barclay 84009)
Tyner	McCoy	McCoy Tyner-Supertrios (April 1977, Milestone-2LP's, M-55003)
Udolph	David	Playing (cdbaby.com)
Uhart	James	Time Away (cdbaby.com)

Urtreger	Rene	Chet Baker in Paris Volume 2(Oct.1955, Emarcy 837475)
Us	Namely	Namely Us (cdbaby.com)
Uvezian	Avo	Legacy (cdbaby.com)
Valdes	Jesus 'Chucho'	Solo Piano (1991, Blue Note CDP780597-2)
Valdes	Bebo	Bebo Rides Again (Nov.1994, Messidor)
Valera	Manuel	Melancolia (cdbaby.com)
Van Dijk	Louis	Trilogy (1975, CBS 80527)
Van Hove	Fred	Flux (Jan.15-16, 1998, Potlatch)
Van Roon	Marc.	Falling Stones (4/94, Mons 874 669) CD
Vander	Maurice	Don Byas: Lover Man(May 10, 1955, American Jazz in Paris)CD
Van't Hof	Jasper	Solo Piano (10/87, Timeless SJP 286)CD
VanVermeulen	Robert	Pictures of Amsterdam(7/95, A Records AL 73042)CD-Amsterdam Jazz Quintet
Varela	Dante	Cosa Nueva-Dante Varela and His Amigos(1962, Rexford, LPM-5014)
Varozza	Stephanie	Fire & Grace (cdbaby.com)
Varro	Johnny	Sittin' In (Oct.8, 1985-July 1995, Too Cool)
Vaughn	Father Tom	Joyful Jazz-Father Tom Vaughn (Concord, CJ-16)
Verlinde	Eric	Peace (cdbaby.com)
Vernon	James	J.V.Trio-House of Jazz (cdbaby.com)

Vicari	Andrea	A.V. Suburban Gorillas (1994, 33 Records)
Viggiani	Carl	Music for Piano and Drums (cdbaby.com)
Vigoda	Bob	Joyce Carr-Vocals (1981, Audiophile, AP-148)LP
Villegas	Enrique	Introducing Villegas (Columbia, CL-787)
Vintskevich	Leonid	Rec. for Russian Melodiya Label
Voerkel	Urs	S'Geschank (5/76, FMP 0300)
Vollenweider	Dale	My Turn (cdbaby.com)
Voynow	Dick	Riverboat Shuffle (1924, Gen. 5454)
Vuckovich	Larry	City Sounds, Village Voices, Palo Alto Jazz
Wackenhut	Fred	Gene Terramani: Hotel Eden (1993, 101 South Records)
Waldo	Terry	Wizard of the Keyboard (July 22-24, 1980, Stomp Off)
Waldron	Mal	Crowd Scene (6/10/89, Soul Note 121218)
Waldron	Rick	Endless Pursuit (cdbaby.com)
Walker	Kit	Freehouse (cdbaby.com)
Wall	Dan	Off The Wall (7/96, Enja ENJ 9310-2)CD-o.
Waller	Fats	Memorial No.2- RCA-Black & White
Wallgren	Jan.	Standards and Blueprints (4/87-2/93, Dragon DRCD 246)CD
Wallin	Per Henrik	Dolphins, Dolphins, Dolphins (8/91, Dragon DRCD 215)CD

Wallington	George	The Workshop of the George Wallington Trio (Norgran 10", MGN-24)
Walter	Cy	Holiday For Keys-Cy Walter (Columbia 10", CL-6202)
Walters	Peter	Portraits in Ivory, Decca-45RPM
Walton	Cedar	Piano Solos (c1981, Clean Cuts 704)
Warner	Scott	Mindfield (cdbaby.com)
Warren	Ernie	An Evening in Peacock Alley-Waldorf Ast.(Everest, SDBR 1033)
Washington	Buck	Old Fashioned Love (1934, Col.2925D)also singer & trumpeter
Washington	Freddie	Barney's Bounce/ Lulu's Mood (1944, Cap. 10022)
Watanabe	Mari	Old Friends (cdbaby.com)
Watkins	Brent	The Heroes of Parlor Town-Vol.1 (cdbaby.com)
Watson	Eric	Yours Tonight Is My Tomorrow (5/87, Owl 047)CD
Watson	Jim	The J.W.Trio, The Loop (cdbaby.com)
Weatherford	Teddy	Tea for Two/Weather Beaten Blues(1937, Swing 5)
Webb	George	Dixielanders (1946, Jazzology) Piano, Leader
Wechsler	Moe	Moe Wechsler Plays Barrelhouse (Roulette, R-25002)LP
Wedgwood	Olly	Just Friends (cdbaby.com)
Weed	Tad	Soloing (7/90-5/91, 9 Winds NWCD 0148) CD
Weed	Buddy	Piano Moods-Buddy Weed (Columbia 10", CL-6160)

Weidman	James	All About Time (cdbaby.com)
Wein	George	G.W. and The Newport All Stars (1993, Sony) Piano, Impresario
Weinbeck	Benny	Solo Piano Standards (cdbaby.com)
Weingart	Steve	Life Times Vol.1 (cdbaby.com)
Weiskopf	Joel	The Search (Criss 1174) CD
Weiss	Michael	Presenting Michael Weiss (4/86, Criss Cross Jazz Crisis 1022)CD
Weldon	Nick	Lavender's Blue (1994, Verge 001)CD
Wellstood	Dick	Jazz at the New School, Chiaroscuro
Werking	Jon	Folk Prayer (cdbaby.com)
Werner	Kenny	Press Enter (8/91, Sunnyside SSC 1056D)CD
Wesseltoft	Bugge	It's Snowing On My Jazz (10/97, Act 9260-2)CD
West	Bobby	Hip Prophecy (cdbaby.com)
West	Tom	Mixology (cdbaby.com)
Westbrook	Mike	Off Abbey Road (8/89, Tip Toe 888805)CD
Weston	Randy	Zulu-Randy Weston (1955-56, Milestone 2 LP's, M-47045)
Whart	James	Camels Dance (cdbaby.com)
Wheals	Tim	Boogie Woogie: Echoes of the Left Hand (cdbaby.com)
Whitaker	Harry	Harry Whitaker Trio-The Sound of Harry Whitaker (cdbaby.com)

White	Sonny	M. Mezzrow: That's how I Feel Today (1937, Vic. 25636)
White	Jerry	J.White's Select Songs (cdbaby.com)
Whitfield	Lon Calvin	Instruments of Praise (cdbaby.com)
Whittington	Dick	In New York (10/86, Concord CCD 4498)CD
Wiggins	Gerry	Gerry Wiggins: Wig is Here (March 1974, Classic Jazz, CJ-117)
Wilcox	Eddie	Flaming Reeds and Screaming Brass/While Love Lasts(1933,Col.CS9515)
Willan	Maxine	Alone and Together (cdbaby.com)
Williams	Al	Buck Clayton: Copenhagen Concert (1959, Ste. 6006-7)
Williams	Clarence	Duos with Bessie Smith:Down-hearted Blues(1923,Col.3844)
Williams	James	Progress Report (1985, Sunnyside 1012)
Williams	Jessica	J.W. at Maybeck-Volume 21, Concord,CCD4525
Williams	Maceo	Slim Gailard-Laughing in Rhythm: Best of the Verve Yrs.('47-52, 314521651-2)
Williams	Rod	Destiny Express (7/90, Muse MCD 5412) CD
Williams	Sidney	Ragtime Piano Interpretations (Folkways RF 24)
Williams	Valdo	New Advanced Jazz (12/66, Savoy SV 0238)CD
Williams	Michael	M.W. with 140 420: west (cdbaby.com)
Williams	Marty	It's No Illusion (cdbaby.com)
Williams	John	The John Williams Trio (Emarcy, MG-36061)

Williams	Mary Lou	Mary Lou Williams-Live At The Cookery (Chiaroscuro, CR-146)
Williams	Roger	Roger Williams-Piano Solos & Duets with Strings & Orch. (Kapp, KL-1012)
Williamson	Claude	C.W. Trio-All God's Chillun Got Rhythm (1977, SeaBreeze, SB-1003)
Willis	Larry	How Do You Keep The Music Playing(4/92, Steeplechase SCCD31312)CD
Willoughby	Harold	Ragtime Piano Interpretations (Folkways RF 24)
Wilner	Spike	Late Night:Live at Smalls (cdbaby.com)
Wilson	Alex	Afro-Saxon (1998, Candid BCCD 79201)CD
Wilson	Buster	Blues For Jimmy (8/3/44-CPM 1034-2: Crescent 2)Side 67B-Franklin Mint Jazz
Wilson	Garland	Sweet Georgia Brown (1951, HMV B10413)
Wilson	Jack	Ragtime Piano Novelties of the Twenties (Folkways RBF 42)
Wilson	Lisette	Unmasked (Atlantic)
Wilson	Gini	Left Coast Local Time (cdbaby.com)
Wilson	Jack	Jack Wilson-Innovations (Aug.1977, Discovery, DS-784)
Wilson	Teddy	Moonglow-Teddy Wilson (June 1987, Black Lion, BL-177)
Winkler	Mark	M.W. Sings Bobby Troup (cdbaby.com)
Wireman	Mike	Too Smooth (cdbaby.com)
Wisner	Jimmy	Apperception-Jimmy Wisner Trio (Chancellor, CHJ-5014)
Wissels	Diederik	Tender Is The Night (1990, B Sharp CDS 075)CD

Witkowski	Deanna	Wide Open Window (cdbaby.com)
Wodrascka	Christine	Vertical (6/95, FMP CD 79)CD
Wofford	Mike	Afterthoughts-Mike Wofford (Jan.1978, Discovery, DS-784)
Wolfe	Neil	One Order of Blues-Neil Wolfe (Imperial, IR-9192)
Wolff	Mike	Cannonball Adderley: Phenix (1975, Fan. 79004)
Wonder	Steve	Songs in the Key of Life, Tamia
Wongozi		Sounds of a New World Afrikah (cdbaby.com)
Wonsey	Anthony	A.W. Quintet- Open The Gates (Criss 1162) CD
Wood	Juli	J.W.,Earma Thompson: Blues For Earman Jean (cdbaby.com)
Wood	Charlie	Somethin' Else (cdbaby.com)
Wooding	Sam	Pianist & comp.; Shanghai Shuffle (1925, Vox)
Woods	William	Every Part Of Me (cdbaby.com)
Woodworth	Liz	Green Lily (cdbaby.com)
Worsdale	Maggie	Joy (cdbaby.com)
Wortham II	Eric D.	When I Became Myself (cdbaby.com)
Wright	John	South Side Soul (8/60, Original Jazz Classics OJC 1743)CD
Wright	Marvin	Boogie Woogie Piano-Lefty Wright ("X"-RCA 10", LXA3028)LP
Wright	Pearl	accompanist for singers

Wright	Clayton	Moondust (cdbaby.com)
Wrightsman	Stan	Pete Fountain on Tour (1961, Coral 57337)
Wu	Alex	Alex Wu & Frank Ponzio- Duo Piano Concert (cdbaby.com)
Wyands	Richard	Then, Here And Now (10/78, Storyville SLP 4083)
Wyeth	Howie	Chadds Ford Getaway (cdbaby.com)
Yagi	Masao	M.Y. Plays Thelonious Monk (1960, King 3014)Pianist,composer,arranger
Yahel	Sam	o-Searchin' (4/96, Naxos Jazz 860004)CD
Yamashita	Yosuke	f- Sentimental (1985, Kitty H33K20018)
Yancey	Jimmy	At the Window (1943, Session 10-005)
Yenana	Andile	We Use To Dance (cdbaby.com)
Yoshizawa	Hajime	Hajime (12/90, ah um 008) CD
Young	John	J.Y. Trio- Themes and Things, Argo
Young	Larry	o- Spaceball (1975, Ari. 4072)
Z	Rachel	Trust the Universe (1993, Columbia)
Z	Laurie	Roots, The Solo Piano Album (cdbaby.com)
Zack	George	That Da Da Strain (7/7/39-040263-2 Bluebird 10384) 67A-Franklin Mint Jazz
Zarathustra	Miles	Dragon & Bodhisattva (cdbaby.com)
Zawinul	Joe	Zawinul (1970, Atl. 1579)

Zee	Bobby	Piano After Dark (cdbaby.com)
Zeitlin	Denny	At Maybeck:Volume 27 (10/92, Concord CCD 4572)CD
Zerbe	Hannes	Rondo A La Fried (3/92, Bvhaast CD 9207) CD
Ziegler	Pablo	Pablo Ziegler Quintet for new tango (Feb.3, 1999, RCA)
Ziegler	Ken	Water Wheel (cdbaby.com)
Zimmer	Jerry	Blame it On My Youth (cdbaby.com)
Zimmerman	Roy	(Monk Hazel - South. 217)
Zingg	Silvan	S.Z. Trio- Boogiewoogie Triology (cdbaby.com)
Zito	Torrie	CD's w. Merrill (Verve, JVC, Par)
Zoller	Dave	Love Song to a Genie (cdbaby.com)
Zoo	Alameda	Objects in the Rear View Mirror (cdbaby.com)
Zumbrunn	Karen	K.Z.Trio-Twilight World (cdbaby.com)
Zurke	Bob	B.Crosby: Fidgety Feet (1937, Decca 1593)
Zwingenberger	Axel	Boogie Woogie Live (Vagabond VR 885007)CD

About the Author

Arnie Fox was born in 1941 in Philadelphia, PA. He graduated from Drexel University with a B.S. in accounting and later was in the insurance and investment business for twenty-nine years. He retired in 1997 and plays for over 200 different nursing homes and assisted living facilities throughout the year. In addition, he performs at weddings, parties and cocktail lounges. He prefers performing for the senior citizens, because many residents greatly appreciate the music, and share his love for the "old standards".

Arnie Fox is primarily a self-taught musician. After twenty years, he decided to take lessons for ten months. He has been playing the piano and keyboard for over forty years, and has been playing professionally for more than twenty years. He describes himself as primarily a singer, jazz and pop musician who enjoys playing the music of George Gershwin, Duke Ellington and Cole Porter.

He has collected records for most of his life and has over 3000 albums and CD's which are mainly vocals and jazz piano. He is always looking for that new jazz pianist.

He resides in Bucks County with his wife, Diana and daughter, Pamela and their two cats, Inkspot and Tyger.

NOTES

Lightning Source UK Ltd.
Milton Keynes UK
15 October 2010

161341UK00001B/19/A